Game Design
Deep Dive

Game Design Deep Dive

Platformers

Joshua Bycer

CRC Press

Taylor & Francis Group

Boca Raton London New York

CRC Press is an imprint of the
Taylor & Francis Group, an **informa** business

CRC Press
Taylor & Francis Group
6000 Broken Sound Parkway NW, Suite 300
Boca Raton, FL 33487-2742

International Standard Book Number-13: 9780367211387 (paperback) 9780367211417 (hardback)

Visit the Taylor & Francis Web site at
www.taylorandfrancis.com

and the CRC Press Web site at
www.crcpress.com

Contents

Acknowledgments

For the months I spent writing this book, I had a special offer for my fans and supporters. For anyone who donated a select amount to my patreon (http://patreon.com/gwbycer) or via online donation, they received an acknowledgment in this book. Keep an eye out for future works of mine, as I'll be making similar promotions there. Without further ado, I would like to thank the following people for contributing that helped me to focus on this book:

Charles Currer

D.S.

Mike M. Garcia

Robert Leach

Irish Mojo

Foreword: A Game Design Deep Dive into Platformers

Some of the most fascinating parts of game design occur at the individual layer of **mechanics** or **systems** that become the basis for a title. Far too often, new designers will approach a design and not understand the depth that separates the great titles from the not so great. For that reason, I wanted to create a new series of books called "Game Design Deep Dive" to shine a light and explain how simple actions can have complex designs.

And what better place to start with than one of the first game mechanics to achieve popularity? Jumping has been around since the early 1980s, and for a time, the **platformer** genre was the most popular and developed in the industry.

Jumping is a mechanic that looks very simple to design – with many first-time developers making their first game a platformer. As we're about to discuss in this book, there is a lot that goes into making the mechanic feel right in the **player**'s hands.

I hope you enjoy this book, as there are plenty more topics to examine in future design dives. As always, please let me know what you think about the book at josh@game-wisdom.com.

1

The Legacy of Jumping

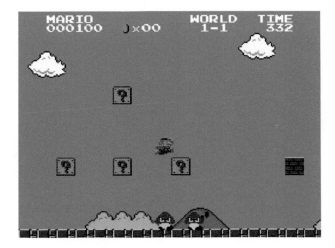

Jumping, and by extension, platforming, have been around for over 30 years. It is the genre that kick-started Nintendo's dominance of the console market; it was the most popular genre of game being developed in the late 1990s; and it still has relevance to this day.

For a lot of students and first-time developers, just being able to get a character to jump is the game design equivalent of getting a program to output "hello world." Considering how much game design has evolved, it's easy to look at platforming and jumping as being basic elements, and that is why this first book in this series is dedicated to it.

The line between the very best and very worst platformers is very wide, and it can be hard for designers and consumers to understand the difference.

1.1 The Timelessness of Platforming

When we look at the growth of the game industry, it's easy to think that jumping and platforming are holdovers of a bygone era of the industry – like the evolution of transportation from horse carriages to modern cars. Despite all the improvements in graphics, hardware, and game design, platforming remains timeless.

The two philosophies when it comes to progressing through a game are abstracted progression and skill-based. Abstracted progression is commonly seen in **RPGs** as a way for the in-game character to grow. Skill-based is about the player themselves becoming better at the game. Many titles today feature a combination of the two philosophies: such as having leveling up and unlocks in shooters like *Battlefield* and *Call of Duty*.

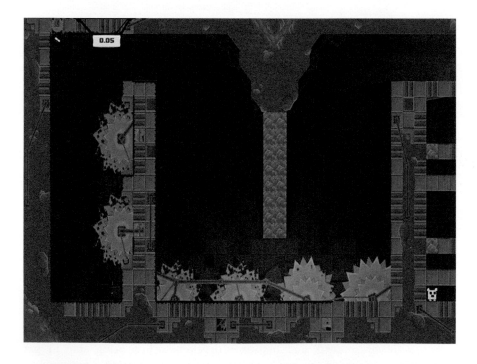

Platformers, along with action titles, are some of the best examples of skill-based design. Playing one, it's all about the player figuring out how to guide their character through the level with no other systems getting in the way. Some of the hardest plat-formers challenge the player to rise up to their level with sections that require him or her to figure out the right path while having the technical skills to perform.

And despite that, there are plenty of platformers aimed at telling a story, and being designed so that anyone can play them.

The genre itself is almost like a blank canvas for someone to put their own unique stamp on, and despite how far the industry has come, it is not going away anytime soon.

1.2 Why Platforming Is Not Going Away

Since the early days when the first platformers were released, outside of Nin-tendo, many of the companies that grew the genre's popularity are either no longer around or not making platformers anymore.

With the rise of cinematic storytelling and blockbuster titles like *Red Dead Redemption 2, God of War, The Legend and Zelda: Breath of the Wild*, and many more, a game that is just about jumping seems old today.

However, like 2D design in general, platformers continue to be a go-to genre for developers for several reasons. First is the simple fact that 2D design continues to be one of the best entry points for new designers.

The implementation of jumping is universal among game design and gamers, making it very easy to pick up. You don't need to spend a lot of time educating the player about what jumping is, and you can quickly introduce the mechanics and systems that make your game stand out.

From a design standpoint, it is far easier to develop and balance a 2D game compared to a 3D one. The simple fact that designers don't have to worry about camera control (something we'll be talking about later in this book) removes a huge technical hurdle for new developers. It is also easier to create an aesthetically pleasing game in 2D than it is in 3D on a small budget. Despite the fact that quality textures and character models will still cost good money, it is nowhere near as expensive compared to a 3D game.

Lastly we have the nostalgic factor. There are plenty of gamers who enjoy retro-inspired titles like *Shovel Knight* – that looks like a retro game, but has modern design elements to it. There are still developers working on games for retro consoles, and the "modern-retro" market does exist out there.

With that said it's time to begin our history lesson: going back to the start of platformers.

2

The First Jumps

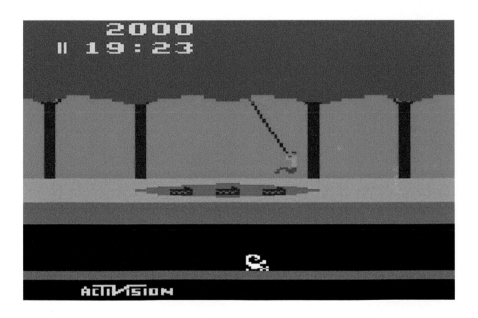

2.1 Defining the Platformer

The use of jumping as a mechanic in a video game did not appear at the start of the game industry. Early video games were played from a top-down viewpoint which didn't allow for any kind of jumping. Even when we started to see platformer-styled games, there were still some discussions about what we call a platformer.

We're not going to be focusing on individual games that much in this book, but it's important to talk about major milestones in platformers and how they created the foundation for titles that featured jumping.

To start with, the term "platformer" originally referred to games where players would climb up or down ladders with platforms between them; without any form of jumping. There were several games released before and after what would become the standard, but since this book is focused on the act of jumping, we won't be spending time on them.

The accepted modern definition of a platformer is a game where the primary mechanic involves jumping – usually over or around obstacles.

In 1981, we would get our first example of true platformer design with *Donkey Kong*.

2.2 Pitfalls and Plumbers

Donkey Kong by Nintendo was influential in the company establishing contact in the USA and their first major success in the arcade industry. Designed by Shigeru Miyamoto and Gunpei Yokoi, it became recognized as our first introduction to Mario before he got his now famous name (in the original version he was called Jumpman). *Donkey Kong*'s design may seem basic today, but it was ahead of its time when compared to the rest of the arcade industry.

In the arcade, *Donkey Kong* was made up of four levels comprising four screens each.

As Mario, your mission was to reach Pauline, or the damsel in distress, while avoiding the obstacles Donkey Kong threw. The player needed to jump over the barrels that would follow the platforms down. Players could use the ladders as shortcuts, but a rolling barrel could roll down the rungs hitting the player.

If the player could reach a hammer, they would gain the ability to destroy barrels at the cost of being able to jump. The hammer was the only way to deal with flames that would appear when blue barrels reached the fire at the bottom of the stage.

The player's ability to jump would be tested in stage three (stage two in the later home version), featuring the first use of moving platforms as an obstacle. The game was also the first platformer to use falling to hurt the player. Falling off a platform at any height would cause the player to lose a life. The use of **fall damage** appears on and off throughout the history of the game industry and platformer genre and we'll return to this topic in Chapter 7.

Donkey Kong, along with other early platforms, made use of **committed jumping** that we'll be talking more about in the next chapter. To briefly define it now, committed jumping means that the player has no control over the character's trajectory once they leave the ground.

A key limitation of *Donkey Kong* compared to platformers to come was the use of fixed screens. With each level only being one screen long, it meant that the game was on the short side. To keep people playing, *Donkey Kong* had

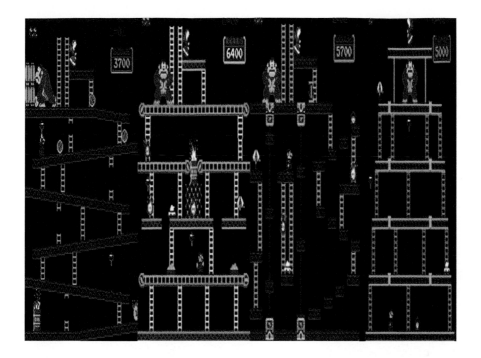

a progressively growing difficulty that increased the speed of the obstacles with every four screens beaten.

The first game to make use of a scrolling screen was Sega's *Jump Bug* released in 1981 after *Donkey Kong*. However, despite the innovation, it did not become as recognized as our next game.

That would be Atari's *Pitfall!*, released in 1982. Despite featuring graphics that looked more primitive compared to *Donkey Kong*, *Pitfall!* had several innovations that would begin to define the platformer genre.

The objective of the game was to guide the hero, Pitfall Harry, through the jungle to find 32 treasures in 20 minutes. The player had 255 screens to go through while dodging scorpions, swinging on vines, and jumping across alligator-infested waters.

Besides being one of the longest games released at the time, *Pitfall!* emulated the idea of side-scrolling screens. Side-scrolling refers to the game not being locked to a single screen, and having the **camera** pan to simulate the character moving through an area. With *Pitfall!*, the game did not use side-scrolling due to it only showing one screen at a time. However, *Pitfall!*'s look would become the foundation for platformers to come.

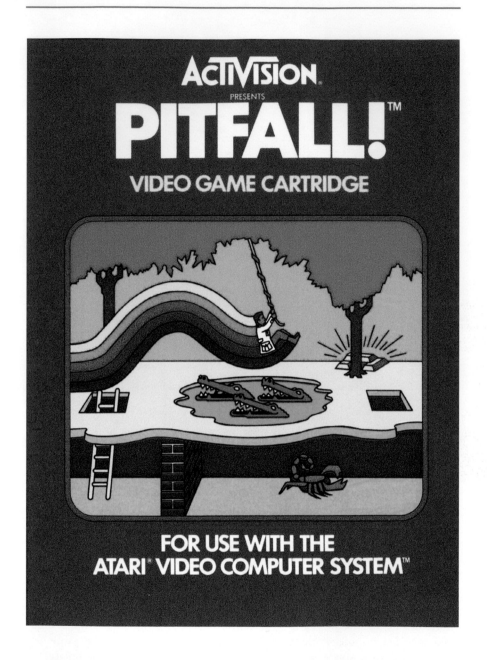

Despite the incoming video game crash of 1983, *Pitfall!*, *Donkey Kong*, and other platformers grew in popularity. With rare exception, early platformers used a form of jumping that I've coined **committed jumping**.

3

Committed Jumping

3.1 What is Committed Jumping?

The simplest form of jumping as a mechanic is committed jumping – where the player has no control over their character once they're in the air. Without direct contact with Nintendo, I can only assume that the reason this was in the original *Donkey Kong* was as a way of mirroring real life jumping.

Of all the ways to implement jumping in your game, committed is by far the easiest. By removing the player's control over their character, they are able to quickly figure out whether or not a jump will be successful. This design extends into the **UI** of the game by only giving the player at minimum two fixed ways of jumping – a standing jump and a moving one.

We'll be talking more about level design and creating the act of jumping in Chapter 6, but for the moment, committed jumping means that the designer knows exactly how far and how high every jump the player will make. From there, it's easy to design the length of gaps and where to place obstacles.

In this regard, committed jumping turns obstacles into pseudo-puzzles – where there is only one intended way to get over the obstacle.

Many developers who are making their first game – or specifically making a retro game homage – will use a committed jumping foundation for their platformer. However, this does present several limitations that must be accommodated in your design.

3.2 Committed Jumping Limitations

Committed jumping severely limits what you can build in a game to challenge the player. Every jump in your game can only be designed around the same exact gap distance, because the player cannot adjust in the air.

From a design standpoint, you want to avoid challenging the player to make a jump onto a small landing point that is less than their maximum jump distance. The obvious solution is that the player must extrapolate where to start their jump to avoid overshooting the landing point. However, this can be punishing to players who lack the ability to figure this out.

For games that put **power-ups** in the air, it can be very frustrating to grab them when there is only a few jumping angles that will hit it. For airborne enemies or those that can only be hurt from an aerial attack, committed jumping can take on a higher level of frustration.

When trying to attack a moving enemy, the margin for error to hit the enemy without taking damage is low. Many times in committed platformers, the player will jump at the enemy and hit them, but they would misjudge the distance and fly into the enemy's **hitbox** and receive damage.

"Movement" is the hardest enemy in committed jumping designs. When you're trying to engage a moving target or leaping onto a moving platform, the player must make multiple mental calculations. This becomes even harder if the ground the player is standing on is also moving at the same time.

The player cannot make any mistakes while jumping, which can lead to tense gameplay. One feature that some games made use of for committed jumping is offering players the ability to "stop" the character in mid-air – preventing the player from overshooting a target or jumping into an enemy and taking damage.

Even though most designers moved away from committed jumping early in the lifespan of platformers, they still had a place in slower-paced games that we will return to when discussing adventure platformers.

One of the most famous examples of committed jumping was the game *Bionic Commando* due to the very fact that the player technically didn't jump. All aerial movement was done by launching the character's "bionic arm" to grapple with the ceiling and swing. While this was, and still is, unique for platformers, the game also embodied all the frustrating elements of committed jump design. Due to the fixed arc of swinging, it was very easy to misjudge the landing on small platforms.

During the 1980s, developers quickly evolved the platformer genre from *Donkey Kong* and its peers, and gave us the second kind of jumping philosophy.

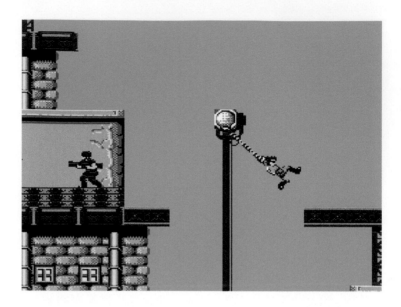

Variable Jumping

4.1 What Is Variable Jumping?

For lack of a widely agreed upon term, I'm going to use **variable jumping**. This is another form of jumping where the player has more control over their character in the air. Instead of being locked into whatever direction the initial jump began in, the player can move left or right within the character's maximum jump range. Unlike committed jumping where there are only two kinds of jumps, variable jumping allows for far more variety based on different variables that we'll talk about in Chapter 6.

Obviously, this is less realistic than committed jumping, but it opened up the door for evolving platforming design, the reason being that the player (and by extension the designer) is not limited to only two locked velocities. Instead, the player is given far more control over where the character will land. Many platformers introduced challenges where the player must quickly jump around or through obstacles that needed to be perfectly timed.

One of the first examples of this would come from Nintendo with *Super Mario Brothers*. Even though Mario's movement in the air was limited, it still allowed for players to adjust his trajectory.

A major part of variable jumping is the idea of **micro-adjustments**, or being able to make slight adjustments in the character's velocity to avoid obstacles.

The use of micro-adjustments has become a staple of expert platformers and the **Kaizo** era of games, which we'll be focusing more on at the end of this book.

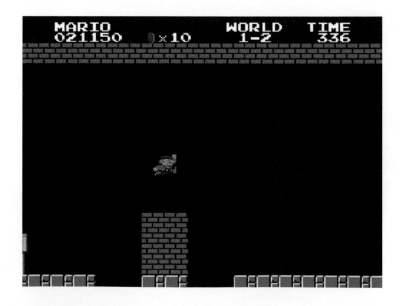

Many of the advanced forms of jumping that we will be talking about in this book required variable jumping to be even possible. Given the importance variable jumping has had on the genre and jumping as a whole, it does beg the question: What's the better form of jumping?

4.2 Committed vs. Variable

Both forms of jumping have become popular in their own ways. Committed jumping is a lot easier for novices to perform, while variable jumping offers players more technical challenges.

If jumping/platforming is not a part of the **core gameplay loop** of a title, a committed system that has fixed jumping and angles can work. As we mentioned earlier, many games built on retro designs or emulating that feel will go with committed.

Variable jumping requires more work on the design side to get the feeling right, and can be harder for new players to learn who didn't grow up playing platformers. We'll be talking more about level design in Chapter 7 and discussing the ways levels can teach the player how to jump. For most gamers, they do prefer variable jumping over a committed system as it has been used in so many titles.

For now, it's time to turn to arguably the zenith of 2D platformer design in the mainstream market.

5

The 2D Mascot
Platformer Era

5.1 Genesis Does What Nintendon't

When most people think about 2D platformers, they will go with a mascot plat-former. The 2D mascot platformer started with the original *Super Mario Brothers* in 1985. Tracking the end of this period is difficult, as major studios were still making 2D platformers into the 2000s, with the torch being passed to indie developers last decade. With that said, we begin with the rivalry that changed the game industry.

The Sega/Nintendo rivalry of the late 1980s into the 1990s marked a monumental period of the game industry, which has been discussed in many other books. These two companies made decisions that would come to impact the game industry to this very day – such as Nintendo causing Sony to develop the PlayStation after cutting them out of a partnership deal.

Both companies put out marquis platformers that set the standards for mascot-driven games. With Nintendo having a head start with the Nintendo Entertainment System (NES) in the USA, Sega branded themselves the oppos-ite of Nintendo, and by extension Sonic vs. Mario.

At the time of *Sonic the Hedgehog*'s release in 1991, Nintendo was ahead in the USA with *Super Mario Brothers 1, 2*, and *3* already out, and *Super Mario World* to be released shortly after Sonic's first game in the USA. We could dedicate entire series of books examining each series, but for now, we want to examine the platforming design.

5.2 Mario's World

Mario's platforming has always been built as a slower, more technical focus compared to Sonic. As mentioned, the Mario series was one of the first to make use of variable jumping to allow players control over Mario's velocity in the air.

One element that has become a subtle standard of Mario games was having variety beyond just the platform levels. *Super Mario Brothers* featured under-water sections, and the infamous puzzle section in the final Bowser Castle. This trend would extend into all future Mario games as a way of breaking up the formula and giving the designers more leeway in terms of creating challenges.

We're not going to talk about the US version of *Super Mario Brothers 2* in this section, and the reason why will be discussed in Section 5.4. *Super Mario Brothers 3* grew all aspects of the design seen in *Super Mario Brothers 1*, including the jumping.

Players had more control over Mario's velocity in the air. Besides having different variations of jumping based on how long the player held the A button, *Super Mario Brothers 3* introduced a new mechanic in the form of "P-Speed." If the player continued to run, they would fill up a meter at the bottom of the screen. Once full, Mario's speed would be faster and he could jump farther than otherwise allowed.

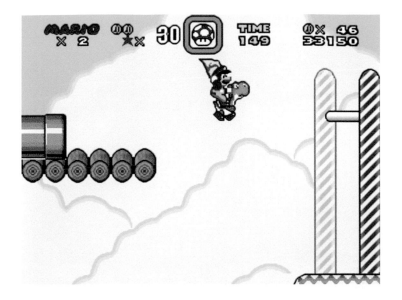

This also factored into one of Mario's most iconic power-ups: the Raccoon Suit. While running at P-Speed and using the suit, Mario could fly through the air until the P-Speed ran out.

Super Mario Brothers 3 was also released at the time when Nintendo began to experiment with level and world themes. Each world in the game had a different theme to it, affecting the enemies, obstacles, and level design. Many situations in the game were locked to their specific world, and sometimes just a level.

The improvements to Mario's design would continue into the first 16-bit outing by Nintendo: *Super Mario World*. Besides massively growing the level design and variety, *Super Mario World* also expanded the number of jumping options for Mario. Mario still had his trademark jump that could be tweaked based on how long the player held the button down for, but this would be the first time that he would be given additional ways alongside it.

Pressing the A button would cause Mario to "spin jump," which had a shorter jumping distance, but unique properties to it. Mario could destroy blocks in his super state, bounce off enemies who would otherwise hurt him, and was faster on the descending part of the jump. This jump also had a shorter minimum height to it – making it easier to dodge obstacles above him.

A new character in the form of Yoshi was introduced. While riding Yoshi, Mario could safely cross certain hazards and could leap off Yoshi for the highest possible jump in the game.

Besides Yoshi, the most iconic addition added in *Super Mario World* was the cape. While equipped with it, Mario's jumping ability changed dramatically. He was able to slow his descent in mid-air – enabling greater control of micro-adjustments and increasing his maximum jump distance.

Given enough running distance, players could fly with Mario's cape, allowing them to bypass entire stages and perform complicated aerial maneuvers. Unlike *Super Mario Brothers 3*, there was no P-Speed to dictate maximum speed. Instead, the designers simplified it to whether or not Mario was able to run a fixed distance to achieve maximum speed. For a greater breakdown of *Super Mario World's* design, check out Patrick Holleman's *Reverse Design: Super Mario World*.

The impact that Mario 1, 3, and World had on platforming design cannot be understated. Despite Nintendo moving to different designs in later games, fans have been taking things further thanks to *Super Mario Maker* and the growth of the Kaizo community (both will be discussed at the end of the book). As Nintendo evolved Mario's design over the 1990s, Sega did everything they could to stand out with Sonic.

5.3 Sonic's Boom

Sonic's adherence to being the opposite of Mario could be seen in every aspect of the game: from his speed, to his mannerisms, and primarily in the level design. Sonic's jumping ability was far more impacted by his momentum compared to Mario. Running at full speed and jumping, Sonic would jump lower in the air, but would cover a farther distance.

Even just slightly moving in either direction would impact the trajectory of his jump. Due to the momentum being carried into the jump, players had less control over Sonic's aerial velocity compared to Mario and other platformers. This would also be the first example of physics impacting a character's velocity in a number of ways, which we will be returning to in Chapter 15.

Due to Sonic's speed being much faster than Mario's, the levels were designed to be longer to compensate. This created an interesting difference between a Mario level and a Sonic level in relation to the platforming.

With Mario, levels were designed as a series of challenges for the player to complete in a set order. The developers knew exactly where the player would be at any given point, and could design challenges in a progressively harder variety.

Sonic's levels were designed around at minimum two different paths for the player to go through depending on their platforming skill. Missing a jump in one path could send the player to the other one without any way of getting back. Many times, the player would lose control of Sonic while he automatically gets "carried" through a section. Depending on how someone played a level, they may never see entire sections and secrets, but all paths converged at the end post.

The chaotic nature of Sonic's levels made them less memorable in my opinion. While players certainly remember obstacles such as the water levels, the overall designs don't stick out the same way as the levels in the Mario series. Sonic's game structure during the 2D era was different as well.

Instead of building a lot of levels around a specific theme, Sonic Team went with just two levels tied to a "zone," with the first Sonic having three.

The zones had completely different backgrounds, hazards, and always ended with a battle with series' villain Robotnik (later renamed Eggman).

In Sonic, the player spends more time running (or rolling) compared to jumping when moving through levels. The focus switches when the player runs into obstacles like platforms, enemies, and hazards. Many bosses and enemies could only be defeated by the player jumping into them at the right time.

Despite Sonic's place in the console wars, most players will agree that the platforming design was superior in the Mario games. It was harder to control Sonic compared to Mario due to the need of building up momentum to make most jumps or run up hills. Trying to calculate Sonic's trajectory based on the speed and direction he was moving was harder compared to Mario. It was easy to misjudge the distance when jumping onto small platforms. The increased speed grew to become a major problem due to trying to create diverse levels and sections.

Sonic Team was stuck between a rock and a hard place. Levels were either so fast that the player could easily skip through most sections, or slowed down so much that the level became boring to go through. Despite having multiple sequels, the level design (and platforming) didn't come close in terms of design evolution to what Nintendo was doing with Mario.

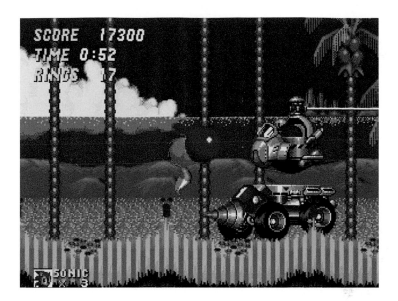

SCORE 17300
TIME 0:52
RINGS 17

SONIC

Sonic Team to this day never figured out how to properly give the player a view to compensate for the increased speed. If the player moved at top speed, there was no way for the average person to be able to react fast enough to dodge obstacles or make jumps (and something we'll be talking about in more detail in Chapter 6). With that said, Sonic was more important to the history of the game industry as it was the first true competitor to Mario, and he would certainly not be the last.

5.4 Mascot Popularity

The success of Mario in terms of worldwide appeal has placed the character in the same realm of brand awareness as Mickey Mouse and Bugs Bunny, and started the mascot platformer trend. Mascot platformers are titles where the player controls a recognizable character – either from an existing property or created for the game. Often times, these games would feature elaborate (for the time) stories to help pull players in.

This kind of branding is different from the 1970s and early 1980s, where players controlled non-descript characters or vehicles. Mascot branding is a major part of advertising, and something far too vast to cover in this book. We were seeing similar trends with cartoons being "toy friendly" with franchises like GI Joe, Teenage Mutant Ninja Turtles, and many more.

The reason why mascot branding took over came down to marketing. People respond better to properties that they recognize. Why should someone play a game with a character they never heard of, when they could play as Mickey Mouse, Aladdin, or even the 7 Up Spot and Domino's Noid.

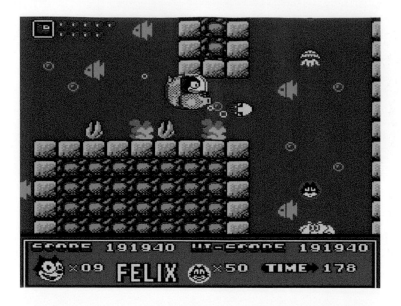

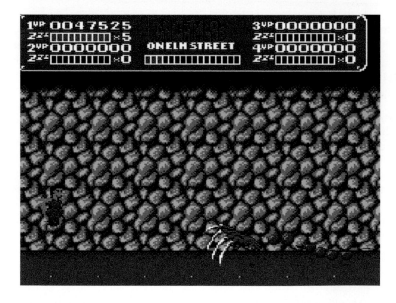

Returning to *Super Mario Brothers 2* for a second, Mario fans know today that Nintendo took the game *Doki Doki Panic* and changed all the character models to the Mario brand to get people to buy it as the supposed sequel in the USA. Japanese players would get a *Super Mario Brothers 2* that was in the

same style as the first game, but featuring harder level design. The USA would eventually get this game in the form of *Super Mario Brothers: The Lost Levels*.

From a franchise point of view, popular characters could have their likenesses used in many other mediums. Licensing various rights off to other companies became as lucrative as the property itself, as fans of *The Simpsons* and *Star Wars* can attest to.

Despite Nintendo holding on to their game rights in the 1990s (except for that ill-fated partnership with Philips), they were more than happy to license Mario off to toys, cereals, and the famous *Super Mario Bros Super Show*, and the infamous *Super Mario Brothers* movie.

The console game industry up until the mid-1990s became dominated by mascot platformers on every platform available.

5.5 The Wide World of Mascots

As we entered the 1990s, more properties were getting converted to platformers. Disney struck a deal with Capcom to develop and release some of the best examples of the genre with games like *Ducktales, Darkwing Duck, The Magical Quest Starring Mickey Mouse*, and many more. Many popular animated series and characters for the time were turned into platformers across all the major systems.

We already talked about Mario, but there were original franchises like *Mega Man* and *Castlevania* that were celebrated. And when those series grew popular, they would spin off into other licensing deals – such as the show *Captain N and the Game Masters*.

Despite the high bar from notable developers, there were many platformers released of varying qualities. Platforming became the go-to foundation for any developer wanting to make a video game. Even if the property wasn't inherently known for platforming, that didn't stop developers from turning *The Simpsons, Bugs Bunny,* and even movies like *Nightmare on Elm Street, Home Alone, Lethal Weapon,* and *The Addams Family* into platformers. While some of these games did stand out by their quality or uniqueness, one of the most infamous publishers of licensed games was the company LJN.

They secured numerous licensing rights before and after being acquired by Acclaim to create games from. Their published games lists could be considered the worst collection of games from one publisher until their closure in 1995. The lack of quality in licensed games became a running joke and stigma for consumers that lasted well into the 2000s.

We could spend an entire book chronicling the designs of LJN's most infamous games, but as we continue our talk about good and bad jumping design, keep in mind that a lot of the bad in 2D design came from the mascot era.

Now that we've discussed the history of traditional 2D platforming, it's time to talk design.

6

Basic 2D Design

6.1 Jumping Logic

Welcome to the first of four chapters that focuses on the design of jumping and platformers. These chapters will explore more of the gameplay logic that goes into jumping. For this one, we're going to talk about the basics of jumping that make up every 2D platformer.

Even though this is not a programming book, it's still important to understand the basic principle of implementing a jump. At the simplest level, the character has two states they can be in – a "ground" state and an "aerial" state.

When the character is on the ground, pressing whatever button performs the jumping action will lift the character up in the air dependent on several variables that we'll talk about in Section 6.3. While the character is considered "aerial," depending on the game, pressing the jump button again will not let the character jump again. Likewise, walking off a platform will trigger the aerial state, due to the game checking for whether or not the character is on a surface.

No matter the design of the game, every platformer will feature at minimum two kinds of jumps – a standing jump and a moving one. While jumping is obviously important, the camera plays a crucial role in design and pacing.

6.2 Camera Angles

The next important element of 2D design is the "camera." One of the reasons for the continued popularity of 2D design for game designers is the fact that the game screen and camera are one; as opposed to the camera being a separate entity in 3D design (that we'll be coming back to in Chapter 12.)

With that said, there are still important considerations to understand about the camera. In older 2D games, enemies only existed when they were on

While you can't see it in this image, the enemies all infinitely respawn whenever the camera reaches invisible trigger points

screen due to technical limitations. This meant that the player could not attack an enemy until they were on screen, and they could be "de-spawned" by moving past them. Enemy spawns were set to "trigger" when the camera would pan to certain spots on the level. This often led to enemies being killed and being brought back instantly if the camera was still at the spawn point.

First generation 2D platformers would often lock the screen's scrolling to one direction which meant that the player could not go backwards.

As design and technology evolved, games allowed the player to move in multiple directions and attack (or be attacked by) off-screen enemies. Later titles would also remember if an enemy was killed and would not respawn them if the camera returned to the spawn point.

The camera itself pans in relation to the player's movement and simulates the action of moving through the environment. Good 2D design will keep the character model at about a quarter of the screen's length and on the opposite side of where they're moving. For platforming vertically, the same rules apply along the Y-axis of the screen. When the character changes direction, the camera must also be set up to change the perspective it's showing.

The reason for this kind of positioning is that it gives the player enough view of what's coming to be able to respond. Returning to *Sonic the Hedgehog*, when Sonic was running at full speed, the character model would move to the halfway point of the screen. The position, combined with the speed of the camera pan, made it hard for players to respond in time to obstacles or jumps.

It would have been better to either zoom out the camera, or keep Sonic's position locked to the quarter portion.

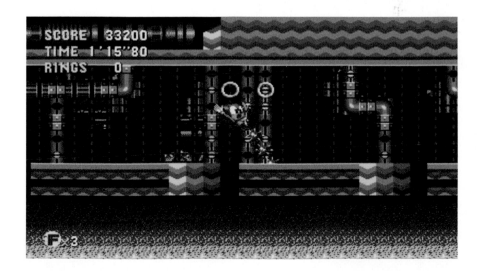

Level design and the camera go hand-in-hand, because the player's only view of the obstacles and level come from the camera. We'll be talking more about level design in Chapter 7, but for the moment, there is a difference in structure between the player only viewing one screen's worth of information at a time, versus the camera continually panning.

It's time to turn our attention to how jumps in platformers are defined and what your options are when creating them.

6.3 The Factors of Jumping

Jumping, and by extension platforming, is a form of gameplay built on the player's skill as opposed to RPG progression. The player must learn how the character will behave in the air to extrapolate the correct timing and movement. To facilitate that, it's important from a design point of view to understand that jumps are fixed elements hard-coded by the game engine. Pressing the jump button the same way 1,000 times should get the same velocity every time.

While that may seem limiting at first glance, there are many ways from a design point of view to impact jumping, and even create different variations of jumping (as we'll talk about in the next section).

The following variables are the DNA of every jump in every platformer ever made:

- Jump Delay;
- Jump Max Height;
- Jump Minimum Height;
- Jump Canceling;
- Jumping Ascending Speed;
- Jumping Descending Speed;
- Committed or Variable;
- Momentum;
- Horizontal Movement Speed;
- Number of Additional Jumps;
- Jump Distance.

While this book is focusing on jumping, it's important to briefly mention how running impacts the player's ability to jump. The faster the player is moving on the ground, the greater the momentum they bring to the jump. Some titles have fixed movement speeds, whereas more complicated titles will use physics to constantly impact the player's speed. If the player achieves top speed too quickly, then it becomes harder to control their character. On the other hand, a character can feel sluggish if it's the other way around.

For each factor outlined above, we can look further at what they can impact when it comes to jumping and the general design of your title.

Jump Delay. This occurs if there is any delay from when the player presses the jump button until the character performs the action. The delay itself is usually represented by the animation of the character preparing to jump, but could sometimes just be the character taking a few milliseconds before leaping. Committed-based jumping will typically have a grandiose animation which is a part of adventure platformers. For variable games, jump delay is looked down upon, as it makes it harder to time more difficult jumps with the additional factor.

Jump Max Height. This determines the maximum height that the character can reach. When combined with horizontal movement speed and jumping descending speed, they will create the maximum distance the character can jump. Once the character hits their maximum height, the descending speed will take over.

Jump Minimum Height. The lowest height a character can jump. This determines how low you can make obstacles for the character to jump below. The quickest jump a player can make is just tapping the jump button and letting go.

Jump Canceling. Can the player stop the jump while the character is ascending? Combined with the ascending speed this allows the player to jump at different heights. When the player cancels their jump, the jumping descending speed will take over.

Jumping Ascending Speed. This is the rate at which the character will reach their maximum jumping height. The slower the player ascends affects the avoiding of obstacles. If the player is allowed to cancel the jump while in the air, this will in turn create multiple jumps for the player to use.

Jumping Descending Speed. How fast does the character fall after they have finished descending? This affects dodging obstacles as well as the maximum jump distance. Some titles will purposely slow the descending speed slightly if the player is still holding the jump button down once the character has begun to descend to give them extra distance.

Committed or Variable. As we mentioned in previous chapters, this concerns the decision to allow players to control the character while they are in the air or not.

Momentum. When the player is in the air, will their character continue to move without further input, or will the direction need to be held the entire time? While it is realistic for momentum to carry the player, this does lead to increased difficulty for the player having to sometimes fight the momentum while controlling their character. This is only a factor if the game features variable jumping. Note: momentum has no impact on the jumping distance.

Horizontal Movement Speed. This is the rate at which the character moves while in the air; when combined with the other factors it will determine the maximum jumping distance.

Number of Additional Jumps. How many times can the character jump while they are in the air? This is used in advanced platformers to add greater challenge to the design. Some games allow the player to gain or recover jumps by doing a specific action (killing an enemy in the air for example).

Jump Distance. This is the total length that a character can jump and is affected by the other variables mentioned. It determines how far gaps should be and balances all obstacles in your game. The closer you make the distance of gaps to the jump distance, the harder it will be to make those leaps. Older platformers sometimes placed ledges just at the edge of the maximum possible jumping distance, requiring players to time their jump perfectly to succeed. The character's maximum run speed will also determine the maximum jump distance.

These variables are locked from a design standpoint and each one will have dramatic impacts on the design and balance of your game. Even though that may seem limiting, with enough creativity, there is plenty of room for making your jumping and platforming different.

6.4 Creating Multiple Jumps

While the attributes that determine how jumping work are fixed, how you use them is entirely up to you, and this has led to a variety of jumping styles over the years. For instance, the first recorded use of a double jump came in 1984 by Namco in the game *Dragon Buster*. If you allow the player to control the descending speed, you can create a gliding or hovering effect as we saw in *Super Mario World 2 Yoshi's Island*.

A famous example of altering jumping properties comes with underwater sections. In the Mario series, the player is essentially allowed to jump infinitely with a slower ascending and descending rate. However, *Mega Man* went a different way. In the water, the player is able to jump as far up as the water with a slower descending speed.

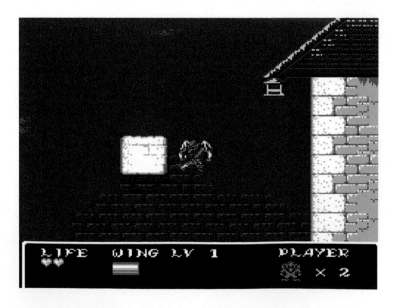

An interesting take on multiple jumps was the game *Gargoyle's Quest* for the NES. Besides giving the player a standard jump, they were also able to fly in the air for a set period of time. Throughout the game, the player would receive upgrades that would augment their ability to jump.

In our previous chapter talking about *Super Mario World*, we discussed how Nintendo gave Mario two different jumps – his normal jump and the "spin jump." This was a rare case of a platformer having jumping actions mapped to two different buttons.

Depending on the complexity of the design, platformers of the 1990s went in one of several directions for their jumping.

1. Variable jumping, with the character only having one fixed jump height;
2. Variable jumping with the character having a high standard jump, and a slightly higher one while holding down the button;
3. Variable jumping where the character has a high maximum jump height and can cancel out at any time.

When you apply other buttons and actions to the act of jumping, even more combinations can be created. While we will be talking about 3D design later in this book, the 3D Mario games each feature multiple jumps based on different factors and button presses.

With *Super Mario 64, Galaxy 1* and *2, Sunshine*, and *Odyssey*, Mario expanded his jumping to (but not limited to) spin jumping, back flipping, wall jumping, triple jumping, long jumping, diving, horizontal flip, and much more.

Speaking of wall jumping, there are multiple properties that go into just that one kind of jumping – to the point where we could even dedicate a section just to it. To be complete, wall jumping is the act of pushing off a wall in the same way as a character jumps off a ground surface. Some games allow the player to "jump up" walls parallel to each other.

Depending on the player's horizontal speed, it could be possible to jump up just one wall, as is the case with titles like *Super Meat Boy* and *N++* (both will be talked about later in the book).

If you're going to make use of additional jumps that are tied to button combinations, it's important to have something in-game to reference that. Some older titles gave the player an enhanced jump that could only be performed by holding down on the controller for a second, or pressing both up and the jump button.

In the platformer *Tom and Jerry*, Jerry has a higher jump that could only be performed by pressing the jump button just after he lands from a regular one. One of the most infamous examples came from the game *Batman Forever* that is the only game I'm aware of that tied the select button to a jump command. These kinds of jumps would not be figured out by someone who was just trying to learn the game.

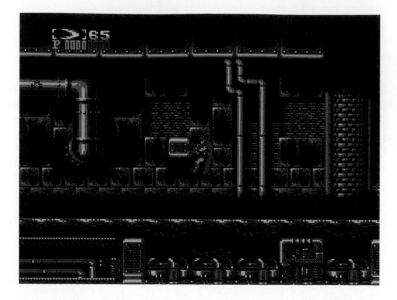

The kinds of jumping in your title will impact the level design of your stages. Any tweaks made to the jumping in your title will often require the levels to be redesigned in order to accommodate them. As an example, if you increase the player's maximum jump distance, then all gaps will have to be widen if you want to keep the game challenging.

Now that we've gone over the basics of jumping, it's time to talk about what someone is going to be using it for.

7

Advanced 2D Design

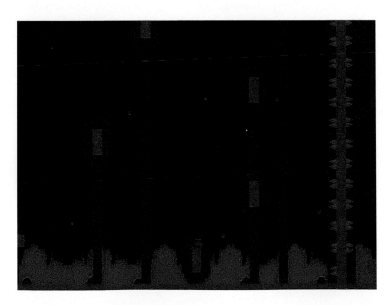

7.1 Level Flow and Structure

Levels in platformers are typically broken down into **sections** that represent a collection of obstacles the player must get past before they are considered safe. Some games allow the player to **checkpoint** after any section is complete, while others will make use of specific areas that save the player's progress.

The further the player has to go before the game saves the progress typically means that the game is on the harder side of platforming. It's considered fair in today's market that if your level goes on for more than a few minutes to include at least one checkpoint.

To keep things streamlined, we're going to refer to a section as the sum total of obstacles before the player's progress is preserved via a checkpoint. There is no limit to the number of checkpoints you want to include in your game, but the less progress the player loses when failing usually makes for an easier experience.

In our previous design chapter we brought up how important the camera is to 2D design. For some games, a section may literally be one screen's worth of obstacles for the player to get past. This kind of design is usually seen in adventure and puzzle-based jumping. As 2D platforming evolved, sections grew to encompass multiple screens and require different kinds of skills.

We'll be talking more about the philosophy of level design in Chapter 17, but for now, it's important to understand that a level typically gets more challenging over the course of the entire level. You don't want to start the level with your hardest situations, as it would upset the flow of the stage. By extension, the **difficulty curve** of the overall game also grows harder from beginning to end.

When it comes to very challenging or unique sections, it's considered good form to have a checkpoint before and after. This way, the player is able to concentrate on doing something very technical and then focus on a new section when it's done.

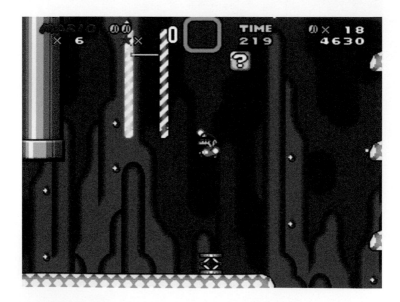

Depending on the game and what kind of challenges you want to test the player on, some end a stage with a boss, while others simply end when the player reaches the end; but there aren't any hard rules when it comes to this point.

In the last section, I referenced the game *Gargoyle's Quest* as an early example of a title that gave the player new and upgrade forms of jumping over the course of play. This kind of practice became adopted by **metroidvania**-designed titles, but there is an important lesson here for level design.

If your game expands the player's ability to jump, and by extension overall movement, then the level design must grow to accommodate the additional features. This can include new obstacles, increasing the spacing between jumping, and much more.

From the outset, the level's design will always be dependent on what kinds of jumps you have in your game. As we get further into this chapter, we'll be talking about obstacle and platforming challenges, and depending on how you designed your jumps, the easier or harder they will be.

Throughout playing your game, the player should be learning how to control their character, and that requires you to teach them.

7.2 Teaching the Player

Without any abstracted elements to get in the way, it's up to the level design itself to educate the player on how to perform the actions needed to win. The platformer genre doesn't need extensive tutorial lessons, and is more about "learning by doing."

This kind of tutorial design is what I've coined an **organic tutorial**, where the game teaches the player through the design of the levels themselves instead of taking them out for a specific tutorial.

Regardless of your game, just about every platformer I've ever played starts with the player simply trying to jump over an obstacle. Ideally, there will be no penalty for failure and the experience is a way for the player to get their feet wet. This kind of "safety net" is typically used when a game introduces a brand new concept or obstacle at any point in the title.

From a design point of view, it's crucial for you to understand the mechanics and techniques needed to play your game. Taking that concept further, you can begin to set up challenges for each of your mechanics in terms of "beginner, moderate, and expert" sections.

It can be hard to break down your sections at that level of detail. It's not just about the complexity of the technique, but the type of challenge you're making. The two key variables to look at is the complexity of the section and the margin for failure you've set up.

If you want to teach something hard to the player, then you want to make sure that they aren't punished for messing up while learning it.

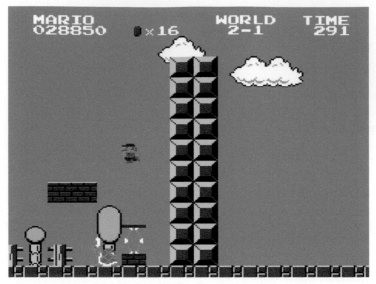

This is the first introduction of the spring mechanic, and it's designed to be a simple as possible for the player to use

The more important a technique is to playing your game, the earlier you should introduce it. If there is a mechanic that requires a specific action to perform it that the player wouldn't figure out through regular play, then you must introduce the player to its existence.

We can use the game *Celeste* as an example. *Celeste* is a platformer that allowed the player to dash in any direction and carry that velocity into different actions. There is a maneuver that requires the player to dash up a corner and perform an extended wall jump. The game makes no mention of its usage during the normal route, even though it would be usable in various situations. It officially gets introduced when players enter the B-side (or extra-hard) set of levels where it's required to win.

7.3 Obstacle Design

Platforming is unique among game genres by providing two kinds of obstacles for the player to deal with. We can categorize them simply by obstacles that the player must avoid or defeat, and having to reach a specific point by jumping to it.

We're going to start with anything that is an active hazard for the player. The most recognizable examples are enemies in a level. Enemy design in any form is far too big a topic to talk about in one section here, and could easily be a future Deep Game Design Dive entry.

When it comes to platformers, there are three kinds of ways of dealing with an obstacle:

1. The player does not interact with it at all and avoids it at all cost;
2. The player has an actual weapon of attack by which they can defeat the obstacle;
3. The player can defeat an obstacle by landing on it while jumping.

Obstacles that fall into the first group are the most common in the platformer genre. The most famous example would be the ubiquitous "death pit" – where the player would fall off screen and lose a life. Older games that made use of vertical scrolling tended to turn the bottom of the screen into an ever present death pit for the player to avoid. Another popular form was the use of "spikes" to denote an area that would kill the player if they touched any of them.

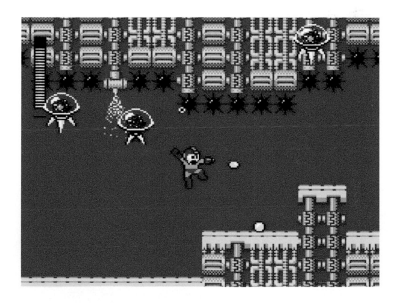

In platformers where the player has no means of attacking an enemy or defeating an incoming obstacle, their only option is to jump over it. The model's hitbox in relation to the character's maximum jump height impacts the difficulty of this.

Weapons in platformers can either be infinite, such as in *Contra*, or the player has to keep picking up power-ups to refill.

The idea of bouncing off an enemy in a platformer was first seen in *Super Mario Brothers*, but we could also count the hit arcade game *Joust* as an earlier example. In the game, players rode flying ostriches and whoever was higher upon impact would win.

With the wide range of platformers released, some allowed the player to defeat enemies this way, while others didn't. This could often lead to mechanic confusion by the player if they played a variety of titles. If your game has enemies that you can and cannot defeat by jumping on them, then you need to make some kind of visual distinction between the two – such as Mario's "spiny" enemies.

Regardless of the obstacle, a big distinction in platformers comes down to the number of hits the player has to take to lose a life. The more chances the player has, the easier the game would be. Advanced play in titles where the player can take multiple hits is to purposely take damage, or to "damage boost" their way through harder sections.

With that said, many platformers will feature obstacles that are instant death no matter what; such as the death pits mentioned above.

7.4 Platforming Challenge Design

Obstacles that the player must use jumping in some capacity are more apt for this book for obvious reasons. Despite platformers and jumping being around for so long, the number of ways of challenging the player is limited. The ultimate goal of the player is to use their understanding of the mechanics and physics of the game to extrapolate the correct jump to reach the next piece of ground.

When it comes to creating a jumping-based obstacle, there are only three areas as a designer that you can influence the difficulty:

- Where the player is jumping from;
- What the player is doing in the air;
- Where the player has to land.

Let's go over each point. Typically the surface that the player is jumping from is static – allowing the player to focus on what they're doing. Messing with the jumping point requires the player to process additional factors and increases the difficulty (we'll go into more detail in the next section).

What happens in the air is dependent on the mechanics of the game. The simplest way to add challenge is to have obstacles that the player must avoid while the character is in the air. This can be from dodging projectiles coming at the character, to making sure that they don't hit something above or below the character. Advanced platformers may give the player the ability to double jump or propel themselves a limited number of times. The more elements the player has to manage ultimately adds to the complexity of the jump.

Finally we have the landing point. The basic way to make landing harder is to have the platform or piece of ground moving. The player must figure out the best time to jump by judging the speed of the movement with their own movement in the air.

The size of the landing point is also a factor. The less room for the player to land on can lead to some of the hardest jumps in games. For games that allow the player to bounce off enemies, landing on them creates a one-time platform that the player must use or they will miss their opportunity to keep going.

The more elements at play, the harder it will be for a player to put all that together. With the factors mentioned, we can now discuss some of the hardest forms of jumping and platforming seen in the genre.

7.5 The Hardest Jumps

In the previous section we talked about the philosophy of designing a platforming challenge and the variables that can be tweaked to make things easier or harder. When it comes to making hard jumps, there are several areas of focus that will increase the difficulty, and some famous examples.

A major factor is using the player's own control over the character against them. The player's control can be influenced by requiring a high level of technicality, or using the game mechanics against the player.

Technical challenges require the player to perform very specific actions at the right time in order to win. At the highest level, we can talk about sections that only have one exact motion that will get the player through safely. Many Kaizo games will feature sections made up of constantly different maneuvers that must all be performed exactly as designed, and any slip-up will cost the player the run.

The player's control over their character is a delicate thing, and if they feel like they've lost control – or the character is not behaving how they expect them to – the game experience will suffer as a result. Elements that purposely mess with the player's control are where we get to the hardest kinds of jumps. What you don't want is the UI itself affecting the player's control over their character.

An example would be if the player can't easily cancel out of a jump – leading to many accidents of hitting something above them. A big issue is if the game itself dictates the nature of the jump – such as automatically deciding the velocity of the jump without further input from the player.

With all that said, we're going to discuss some of these challenges seen in platformers from the early days to the modern era.

Blind Jumps

A blind jump is where the player must leap to safety without being able to see their character or the platform they're trying to reach. Oftentimes, these jumps occur when the camera is not properly showing the game space to the player. Some games will purposely design these sections by having on-screen elements that reduce the player's vision, such as darkness or foreground details.

At the moment, Mario is off the top part of the screen

Many older platformers would have the player jump so high that it caused the camera to pan up while they're in the air. The problem was that while the player was in the air, there was no way to also view the platform they were aiming at.

If the camera doesn't pan, then the character will go off screen, and the player will have to figure out where they are without having anything to guide them.

Some titles will have the camera pan up or down depending on the velocity of the player. If the player is moving faster than the camera, you can have situations where the character must be moved, but the camera hasn't caught up yet and the player is going to miss their chance.

A partial solution is if your game features collectible items, such as coins in *Mario*, which can be arranged in a path that the player can follow while jumping blindly.

Character-Wide Challenges

A character-wide challenge is when the player must maneuver around something where the amount of space that is safe is equal to the width of the character, or more specifically their hitbox.

The margin of error is the highest when it comes to character-wide challenges, which is why they are so difficult to perform. The more of these in a row that need to be performed leads to very frustrating challenges.

When trying to jump to or from character-wide platforms, the player needs to be careful not to fall off the platform. An interesting challenge is when the player must make repeated jumps to character-wide platforms in a single maneuver. The reason why is that, depending on the spacing between them, the player will not be able to gather enough momentum from a standing jump to reach the next one in the chain.

We'll be talking about *Super Mario Maker* later in this book, but many designers love to throw in sections of the player maneuvering around character-wide obstacles; sometimes even building the entire level around it.

What makes character wide-challenges so polarizing is that they're not about learning the level or growing in terms of skills, but performing a highly specific set of motions without any sense of mastery or further input by the player. That kind of difficulty can be seen in the next jump.

Pixel Perfect Jumps

When designing the distance of a jump, the more leeway you give the player in terms of how far they need to jump impacts the difficulty. The pixel perfect jump refers to games that set the distance the character needs to cover to be exactly, or almost exactly, the maximum jumping distance.

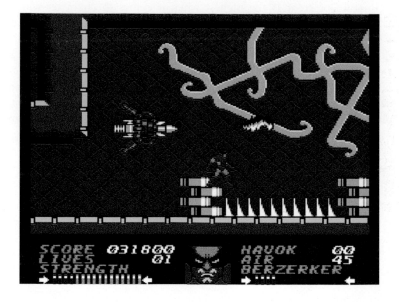

In this situation, there is literally only one way for the player to make the leap. Adding difficulty to these jumps is that it can be very hard to determine how far the player needs to be on the edge before making the leap. Oftentimes, the hitbox of the character is not consistent with the character model itself, leading to cases where the character model can be barely on the edge yet still count.

Many of these jumps end with the player either leaping too soon and not bridging the gap, or waiting too long and the character just falls off the edge without jumping. Similar to character-wide challenges, pixel perfect jumps are harder to balance due to the precision required to complete them.

Bouncy Jumps

As we mentioned above, the player's control over their character is instrumental in figuring out how to get through a platforming obstacle. Our next three examples are when said control is taken away from the player.

The "bouncy jump" is when the player is leaping off a platform that is constantly propelling the player upward. When the player hits the jump button affects their maximum jump height.

The difficulty of the bouncy jump is based on how many jumps the designer has implemented. Some games will only have a few fixed possible jumps from a bouncy platform, and if the player holds down the jump button, they will get the same jump every time.

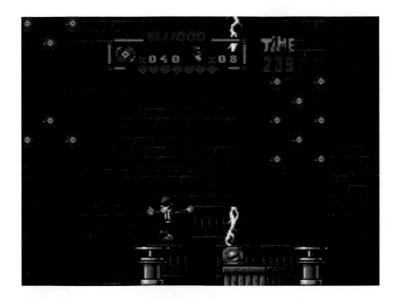

Other games will have multiple jumps all dependent on what position the player is at on the platform. What makes these kinds of jumps difficult is the fact that the player has no control over the platform itself and its impact on the player's jump. Many expert challenges will require the player to make a jump somewhere in-between the minimum and maximum position of the platform. This is further complicated by the speed at which the platform is moving up and down.

Icy Jumps

The second example of when the player's control is taken away from them is performing a jump while dealing with "slippery conditions." Even though icy elements primarily affect ground movement, they can lead to increased difficulty when jumping.

The first point is that when the player is on a slippery surface, their momentum is not completely in their control. From a standing position, this requires more movement to build back up to maximum speed. Once they are moving, it becomes harder to stop and regain control over their character.

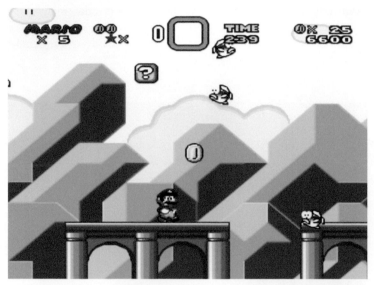

In *Super Mario World*, if any part of the stage is slippery, then all surfaces will be slippery for that stage

Once they are in the air and trying to land somewhere, if the landing point is also slippery, then the character will continue to move once they land. There were platformers released on the NES and SNES where the character may slide instead of coming to a complete stop, or the walk animation would keep going after the player's input has ended, which would also have elements of an icy jump.

Moving Jumps

Trying to figure out the correct jump to make becomes further complicated if the player has to make use of moving platforms. In this case, the player must jump to a platform that is moving either from a still platform or one that is also moving.

The faster the platforms are moving will directly add to the difficulty, requiring the player to account for that speed when jumping. Depending on the physics of the game, the character's jump can also be affected by the speed and direction of the moving platform.

A classic platforming section is when the player must dodge obstacles while returning to a singular moving platform. Not only must the player be avoiding things, but they must keep track of their velocity in the air to make sure that they return to the platform safely. A rare exception to this was in the game *Super Mario World 2 Yoshi's Island*. The player did not need to adjust Yoshi in the air to land back on a moving platform, as the character naturally kept to the pace of the platform.

Trick Jumps

A trick jump is when the player must perform a second (or sometimes third) action while they are in the air. Obviously, the more actions the player must perform in the air, the harder the jump will be. The trick jump category is different from the other ones listed, because it relies on secondary mechanics, which is why we won't spend time describing them in detail. The one factor to keep in mind is how this relates to the control scheme of your game.

If someone is holding the controller in the default position (left thumb on left analog stick, right thumb either on right analog stick or face buttons), you need to be concerned if performing the action will require shifting their hands or putting them in a weird position.

As an example: if the player is already pushing "X" on an Xbox controller, requiring them to hit "B" at the same time will require them to shift their hands into a different position. Not only can this be hard to do in the heat of the moment, but it can start to hurt someone's hands if they have to repeat it constantly.

It's considered good form that the more important a mechanic or action is to the gameplay, the easier it should be to perform at a moment's notice.

Aborted Jumps

The final category is what I call "aborted jumps." The reason most platformers will build their jumps to be less than the character's maximum jump distance is that it allows the player to only worry about the jump from the landing point. If the player goes long, then there will still be ground for them to hit.

This is why one of the hardest kinds of jumps in all videogames is that one which requires the player to "stall" in mid-jump to land on a platform. The player must now not only compensate for the jump itself, but also know when to stop the character's momentum hitting the platform.

Further compounding the difficulty is the fact that once the player stops the momentum, there is no way to get it back, often leading to undershooting the jump. If the character's horizontal jumping speed is too fast, they can easily overshoot the jump if they're not paying attention.

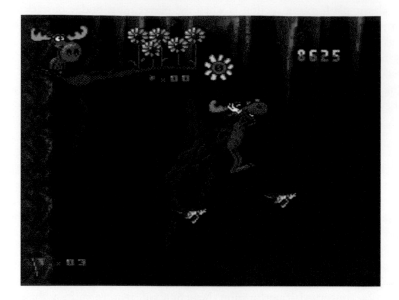

The various jumps that we just described by themselves are harder than normal jumping in a platformer, but they rarely occur individually. To increase the challenge, many platformers will combine these jump types into brutal sections, where the player must make an aborted jump onto a character-wide platform that is also bouncy.

With all that said, what we just talked about are not considered bad design, but simply listing the ways that platforming challenges can be taken to their absolute hardest. In Chapter 17 we'll be talking more about level philosophy and design that allows these challenges to be considered fair instead of frustrating.

One category we didn't cover are elements that change the screen or controls. In *Super Mario World 2: Yoshi's Island*, there is an enemy called a fuzzy. If the player runs into them in a stage, Yoshi will get dizzy, causing the screen to start shifting and Yoshi to start stumbling around. There have also been games where conditions could reverse the controls, flip the camera, and much more.

The reason why we're not covering them here is that they make all aspects of the game harder, and we just want to focus on platforming.

Before we switch topics, I want to return to the topic of fall damage, and how it has become polarizing.

7.6 Fall Damage

Fall damage as we discussed earlier is having the character take damage, or just die, if they fall from too high a distance. This was a popular feature for early 2D platformers, and remains a part of 3D platforming.

Most gamers agree that it's not something they enjoy in 2D platforming, but are willing to accept it in 3D spaces. The problem with fall damage is that it's often seen as throwing salt on the wound. The common occurrence of fall damage happens when the player misses a jump that they were trying to make.

Many 3D platformers give the player an ability that can mitigate any fall damage, such as being able to hover or float

The penalty of having to get back to the position where they need to make the jump is often punishment enough. If you want the act of missing the jump to hurt the player, then you can simply add in environmental obstacles to add danger to the act of missing.

Fall damage is also a binary situation: the second the player falls the designated distance, they will always receive damage. The reason why it's still viewed as acceptable in 3D games is that they offer larger stages, with many titles having platforming sections thousands of feet above ground level.

Another point is that due to the number of ways the character can jump, oftentimes players can cancel the fall damage by performing another action. In the 3D Mario games, simply performing a dive command at the right moment can cancel the fall damage. For 3D adventure games, fall damage typically occurs if the distance is fatal, such as falling from over 50 feet and up.

Moving on, it's time to talk about an interesting fork in the road that some designers went down.

8

The Adventure Platformer

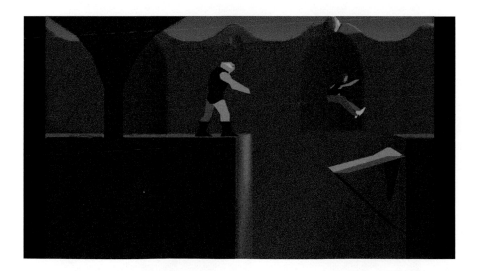

8.1 Story-Driven Jumping

Traditional platformers quickly adopted variable jumping, with rare exceptions like the *Ghost n' Goblins* series. As we referenced earlier in this book, platformers became known for testing the technical skills of the player, oftentimes at the expense to storytelling. However, there is a subsection of platformers that focus more on storytelling and puzzle solving compared to the technicality of jumping.

There isn't an official genre or sub-genre for this category, so we're going to call them "adventure platformers." Adventure platformers will always feature a committed jumping system, and the core gameplay loop is split between platforming and oftentimes one other system, usually combat.

Unlike other platformers where the player is usually conditioned and rewarded for moving fast, adventure platformers are more methodical. Many times, a careless player could run from one screen to the next and get killed due to a trap. Instead of the player being challenged to perform a variety of maneuvers to avoid obstacles, adventure platformers were more about "puzzles."

We'll be talking more about puzzle-based platforming in the next chapter, but let's talk about some of the notable examples.

8.2 Heroic Platforming

The first example I could find that checks the boxes for adventure platforming would be the 1989 game *Prince of Persia*. Designed by Jordan Mechner, the game challenged players to save a princess from an evil Vizier in under 60 minutes. The player had to navigate their way through dungeons while avoiding traps. The other major gameplay system was getting into sword duels with a variety of guards.

While not as plentiful compared to the main platformer genre, we did see other adventure platformers come out through the 1990s. Titles like *Flashback: The Quest for Identity* and *Another World* would define the genre. Perhaps the most recognizable from this era would be Oddworld Inhabitants' breakout hit *Abe's Odyssey* which helped launched the company and their Oddworld branding.

Due to the slower pace and less focus on jumping, we're not going to be spending as much time on this style of platforming, but it's still part of the history of the genre.

8.3 The Pros of Adventure Platforming

Adventure platforming allows players to experience platforming without the need of a high skill level. Since jumping is not the focus, as with traditional platformers, it allows designers to create original sections and challenges with their unique systems.

Many adventure platformers were more story-driven, and removed more of the "gamey" elements such as scoring, lives, and boss fights. The greater focus on storytelling at the time helped them stand out from contemporary platformers that had more over-the-top tales.

The fact that the levels were designed to be shorter and with a slower pace gave designers the opportunity to focus on graphics and aesthetics. While they may not look it now, games like *Another World* and *Oddworld* stood out graphically back in the day.

With that said, adventure platforming has been hit the hardest in terms of popularity thanks to the growth of the videogame medium.

8.4 The Limitations of Adventure Platformers

While adventure platforming did have its time in the sun during the 1990s, its adherence to committed jumping did hurt its long-term viability.

Due to the split focus of jumping paired with another game system, adventure platformers were limited in terms of how much they could stretch their game systems. With variable platforming, you could always keep building things harder and harder thanks to the nature of the design.

Adventure platforms that were locked to only a number of fixed jumps and angles were far more restrictive. There's only so much original content you can make when the player only has a few mechanics to use before you start to repeat. Many adventure platformers had slower movement and animations which led to them feeling clunky to play. Adventure platformers are noticeably shorter compared to variable platforming for this very reason.

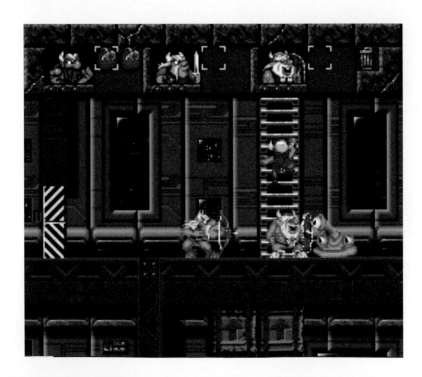

When 3D platformers were developed in the mid-1990s, most of them took the committed design further and combined that with the action-adventure genre. In fact, as storytelling developed across the game industry, adventure platformers quickly disappeared.

As an interesting point, even variable platformers, when we got to the indie era (which we'll be talking about later in the book), would make use of the platforming design, though they paired it with original storytelling. For the concept to work today, the other game system would have to be fleshed out enough to be the focus, and jumping would be the secondary system.

With that said, the use of puzzle-based jumping continues to thrive and has been a part of many 2D and 3D platformers.

9

Puzzle Platforming and Design

9.1 The Thinker's Jump

Starting from the adventure platformer genre, we started to see more games devised with ways of testing the player with platforming instead of through pure skill. Puzzle platforming refers to games where the player must figure out how to move through an area by using the environment or specific items to help them.

The difference between puzzle platforming and traditional platforming is that the focus is on reading the environment as opposed to pure skill. Platforming challenges such as *Super Meat Boy* or *Celeste* would not be considered a puzzle platformer, as even though the player has to figure out the correct way through each section, it is still focusing on technical skill.

Puzzle platforming also gave way to a different form of creating a puzzle that we'll call an **environmental puzzle**. Traditional puzzles are situations that require the player to either perform a specific task or use the correct item and are always pass or fail with no exploration of the games' mechanics. Oftentimes, these puzzles exist separately from the game space or design – such as stopping the game until the player wins a game of tic-tac-toe.

An environmental puzzle is built directly into the game space and challenges the player with a puzzle that is completely in-universe, and often the player may not realize that they're even doing a puzzle. The most popular examples of environmental puzzles are those that require the player to figure out how to get their character to reach a specific point/item or how to get a door open.

Going back to the Oddworld franchise, many of the puzzles not only tested the player on getting the main character through a section, but also **NPCs** that had to be escorted.

In our last chapter we talked about how adventure platforming combined the act of jumping with a secondary mechanic. Puzzle-based platforming will make use of additional systems or rules to devise challenges to test the player. When 3D became the norm in the mid-1990s, many action-adventure titles adopted puzzle platforming as a way of breaking up the combat in those titles. Some famous examples would be *Tomb Raider* and *The Legend of Zelda: The Ocarina of Time*.

We'll be talking about first-person design in our next chapter, but many first-person-based games made use of puzzle platforming. In the hit game *Portal*, the player had to figure out how to use physics to propel themselves through portals to reach the desired areas. *Half-Life 1* and *2* both featured sections where the player's focus is on moving through the environment as opposed to fighting enemies.

Another big difference between puzzle and traditional platforming is with section design. Many 2D games will have a puzzle literally be the size of a single screen. Puzzle-based challenges are smaller than a traditional platformer, with the bulk of the time spent on figuring out what the correct path is as opposed to performing it.

There are several unique challenges to puzzle platforming compared to traditional platforming. From a design standpoint, it is harder to come up with different and progressively more challenging sections to test the player.

The actual platforming itself in these kinds of games is never the focus, which means that you must rely on the secondary mechanics to keep creating

new puzzles. If you don't have enough mechanics to create different situations, then the game will start to feel repetitive.

From a pacing point of view, while the use of checkpoints in traditional games is up for debate, the same can't be said of puzzle platformers. The game should checkpoint every time the player finishes a section. Due to the slower pace of this kind of design, you don't want the player to be repeating content they have already finished.

Another major difference is that, as the designer, you need to understand the two competing elements that go into a puzzle platformer.

9.2 Skill vs. Thought

Puzzle platforming requires both critical thinking and technical skill, which presents an unusual balance for a videogame. Being good at only one will not let the player complete the task, and this can create frustration.

The player can run into a situation where they don't know what the solution is, and they keep performing options thinking that they're just messing things up. On the other hand, the player could know the solution, but they keep running into problems with performing the necessary steps needed to pull it off.

This is why for most puzzle platforming titles, the actual platforming is not as challenging compared to a traditional platformer. The only exception to this rule is when we talk about Kaizo games later on in the book. There are

Kaizo games that make use of puzzle levels – combining technical challenges with a specific order of actions to get through a section.

One way of drastically lowering the difficulty of a puzzle platformer is taking the technical skill requirement out of the equation. In the game *The Swapper*, the player must aim at specific points on the screen while in the air to create clones and "swap" positions with them. Whenever the player is aiming with the swapping device, the game will slow down time to a crawl to allow them all the time needed to perform the action.

Another example would be the title *The Talos Principle* which dealt with first-person puzzle solving and platforming. Whenever the player had to make a jump onto a moving target, they could place the cursor over where they need to jump to, and the game would take over and guide the character to the position.

Depending on the audience that you're aiming for, you need to be mindful as to just how challenging the platforming is going to be alongside the puzzles. If you want the puzzle-solving to be the focus of the gameplay, then you don't want the platforming to require a high technical level.

This can lead to sending mixed signals to your audience – saying that your game is a puzzle title, but requiring skills seen in a challenging platformer.

We've been talking about 2D design over the last nine chapters, but it's time to begin talking about 3D movement and spaces.

10

First-Person Jumping Design

10.1 Jump and Shoot

A **first-person** viewpoint is when the player's viewpoint is literally the camera itself, typically used to simulate the idea that we're looking through the character's eyes. First-person design in and of itself is worthy of being studied – we could dedicate an entire book to it.

The first-person shooter genre much like the rest of the industry can be hard to trace its roots. Older fans will probably say that their first experience was with a game like *Quake* or *Doom*, but there was the precursor to those titles in the form of *Wolfenstein 3D*. Even then, there were older examples of titles that made use of the viewpoint.

When it comes to performing platforming in first person, the oldest example I could find of a game that used the mechanic similar to 2D platformers was the game *System Shock* released in 1994. Many early first-person shooters would have a pseudo-form of jumping. By moving fast enough off an edge, the character could cross gaps similar to a platformer. However, because this was not tied to a command or became a major system, I wouldn't call them first-person platformers.

An interesting point about first-person games is that they featured a unique form of jumping which has been dubbed "crouch-jumping." When the character crouches, their model condenses and takes up less space in the environment. By jumping and crouching at the same time, the character model's legs would be higher off the ground compared to a regular jump. In turn, this allowed players to jump up obstacles that they would normally get stuck at. When first-person games became more realistic in the 2000s, the use of crouch-jumping had all but disappeared in modern shooters.

Jumping in first person is different compared to 2D, or even 3D, design, and has its own set of considerations.

10.2 The First-Person Camera

The biggest difference in terms of design from a 2D title to what we saw with 3D and first person has to do with the camera and information being displayed. In a 2D space, the camera itself automatically tracks the environment around the character – presenting the best viewpoint of the obstacles and level design.

In a 3D space, the camera becomes a controllable element that the player decides what view they will be seeing (for more on camera design in 3D spaces, see Chapter 12). For first-person games, your view is limited to what's directly in front of you.

Playing from a first-person perspective has its own set of unique challenges. As the player, you will never be viewing the entire span of the environment from a limited viewpoint. This means the player has to be constantly turning and adjusting the camera in order to get the information that they need.

If the camera panning is too slow, then it can lead to the player not being able to properly track enemies or make quick movements and jumps. If the camera is too fast in how it moves, this can lead to disorienting the player – with many people suffering from sea-sickness when playing first or third-person titles.

Camera design in first-person titles has not changed since the genre was popularized in the 1990s, and continues to be the reason why first-person platforming is very limiting.

10.3 The Limits of First Person

Despite the evolution of technology and design, first-person gameplay in all forms is always limited by the camera system. When it comes to platforming design, gamers will agree that first-person-based platforming is never as popular compared to 2D and 3D platforming.

There are several different areas where first-person design clashes with platforming. Many first-person titles are built around shooting (hence the genre FPS), these titles tend to focus on high-speed movement that takes into account the character's momentum.

Due to how fast the character is moving, they tend to "slide" upon landing or when they stop running, which we talked about in Chapter 7 with slippery jumps. Without any rails or small walls to stop them, it's very easy for players to jump, land, and then slide right off a platform.

The next issue has to do with the jump itself. To save time in terms of rendering characters and animating, many first-person titles will not show the character's legs when the player looks down. This presents a major problem when it comes to knowing where the character is in relation to any edges the player wants to jump from.

Making matters worse, many first-person titles will not show a shadow under the character. Typically, the shadow is present in 3D games as a way for the player to figure out where their character is within the **gamespace**. Even though first-person games are shown through the viewpoint of the character, without having a shadow or something to reference, it makes precision jumping a lot harder for the player.

If you're going to do a lot of jumping in a first-person game, then you want to give the player a wide berth when it comes to making the jump. Pixel perfect jumping is not recommended due to the frustration factor. It's not uncommon for first-person titles to always have something that will stop the player's momentum once they clear a jump to avoid the sliding issues we mentioned above.

One final issue has to do with the camera itself. As we mentioned, a first-person camera only shows information that the player is directly looking at. This also means the player is not able to quickly turn around to reposition their character as in a 2D or 3D game. Their only option is to rotate the camera in order to realign in a new direction.

Due to how slow camera orientation is, it has a dramatic effect on what kind of obstacles the designer can realistically set up. Challenges that require a lot of camera shifting can be hard on the player's hand to keep turning the mouse, and can once again cause dizziness and sea-sickness in people due to the constant motion. If you're going to have maneuvers that force the player to do a 180-degree turn, you might consider having the camera automatically adjust to make it easier to pull it off.

The three issues we talked about all greatly restrict the kinds of platforming challenges that can be built into a first-person game. The first-person platformers we've seen that focus on platforming tend to be very repetitive in their obstacle design. Similar to puzzle platformers, there are usually secondary mechanics and systems to help keep things from becoming stale.

While first-person platforming hit a wall, 3D would dominate platforming for at least a decade.

The 3D Platformer Era

11.1 Two and a Half D Games

Before 3D was fully adopted, we began to see the use of 3D in a smaller scope; **2.5D** is a style of game that gives a greater illusion of 3D, but still operates on a 2D plane. There are two popular examples of this kind of design.

Many games used **isometric** perspectives to create the illusion of 3D. This was used heavily in strategy and city building games to try and make buildings and units stand out from each other.

The other examples are games that made use of 3D characters in a 2D space, such as the *Donkey Kong Country* series. Later games that made use of 2.5D would sometimes allow the player to move in and out of the plain or depth that they're in to make the world seem larger. One of the first examples of this would be the Sega Saturn game *BUG!*, but it's not a requirement of 2.5D design.

In terms of design, anything that could work in 2D would be fine in 2.5D. From a technical standpoint, it is more work to design a 3D character than it would be a 2D, and is why most 2D platformers still made today tend to stay with a 2D aesthetic, with some exceptions.

There have been platformers that went with a unique aesthetic and the 2.5D really makes it stand out; such as *Ori and the Blind Forest*. While 2.5D has earned its place among platforming fans, it's time to talk about how 3D became the norm.

11.2 The Rise of 3D

As with first-person platforming, trying to find what would be considered the first game of the 3D platformer genre is tough. Developers were experimenting with 3D viewpoints and depth of field as far back as the 1980s. Many of these titles would still have movement restricted, but the viewpoint was different.

During the 1990s, we saw more console manufacturers appear on the scene to try and take the #1 spot away from Nintendo. This also led to a hardware war of each company trying to be the most powerful on the market. From a technical standpoint, the SNES was capable of 3D graphics, but did not have many 3D titles. Sega's add-ons to the Sega Genesis – the 32X and Sega CD – were also powerful enough for 3D. In terms of new competition, we saw the Atari Jaguar and Panasonic 3DO in 1993, along with other handheld competitors.

Part of the challenge of defining 3D platformers was that there were many games that made use of an isometric viewpoint that created the illusion of 3D. The critically acclaimed *Super Mario RPG: Legend of the Seven Stars* made use of that perspective to allow Mario to jump in more directions than just left and right, while *Sonic 3D Blast* allowed players to move him in any direction.

For the purpose of this book, we're going to focus on games that made full use of a 3D gamespace around the player in order to perform platforming challenges. The first game that would technically fit as a 3D platformer would be the 1990 title *Alpha Waves*. In it, players had to maneuver around a 3D world trying to get geometric shapes to reach specific points.

When most gamers think of 3D platforming, the games that would define the genre began to appear in the mid-1990s, with the first 3D platformer of this era also being the first one to be in the first-person perspective: 1995's *Jumping Flash!* for the Playstation 1.

Despite not being the first 3D platformer, the game that would go on to become the blueprint to this very day for 3D platformers would undoubtedly be *Super Mario 64*, and it also was the first title for Nintendo's next successful console after the Super Nintendo: the Nintendo 64.

11.3 The Mario 64 Formula

Mascot-driven games were not slowed down by the development of full 3D. Before Super Mario 64 became the standard, there were attempts by other developers to try and create the next mascot hit before Nintendo appeared on the scene. Following their break with Nintendo, Sony took the, at the time, smaller developer Naughty Dog and published the platformer *Crash Bandicoot* which would become the "mascot" of the Playstation 1 era.

Up until *Super Mario 64*'s release, the early 3D platformers would present themselves in a similar form to 2D games. Gameplay only existed within the levels themselves and there was no real connection from one level to the next.

To say that *Super Mario 64* (or just *Mario 64* from this point on) changed things would be an understatement. If it wasn't for the fact that Mario was so well known, *Mario 64* would have definitely made the list for my previous book, *20 Essential Games to Study*.

There is a lot to cover here, and we'll be continuing the design discussion in the next chapter focusing on 3D elements. From the beginning, *Mario 64* gave us the standard of 3D cameras for platformers.

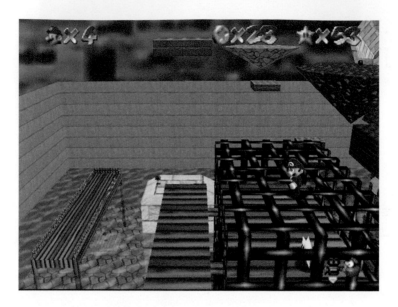

The camera itself would focus on Mario from an almost 3/4 isometric perspective, but would adjust the angle based on the situation at hand. The game would take over the camera at specific obstacles to allow the player to focus on the obstacle at hand and not on orienting the camera. Even though the camera was designed to show the best possible angle, players could still change the elevation and perspective to meet their needs.

A subtle change to the platformer formula was the introduction of the **hub** or over-world. One of the design philosophy changes going from 2D to 3D was trying to build a greater sense of place within the gamespace. Instead of looking at a map or going from one nondescript level to the next, the idea of the hub was to tie everything together into one grand adventure. Some 2D games did have an over-world structure, but nowhere near the depth or complexity as what we would see in 3D.

With *Mario 64*, the game itself took place within Peach's (renamed from Princess Toadstool) castle and the surrounding area. Within the castle there were magical paintings that would transport Mario to a new area/level.

In 2D design, many levels would be tied together, either from an aesthetics point of view or in terms of the types of challenges. With *Mario 64* and the other 3D platformers, there were fewer levels, but they were deeper in terms of the gameplay and design.

Each level in *Mario 64* was essentially a one-off, featuring a different environment, enemies, obstacles, and challenges to overcome. One such level took place in an Egyptian setting, while another was inside a giant clock tower.

A key element of 3D platforming was the idea of collecting a "**mcguffin**" as a form of progression. In *Mario 64*, there were a total of 120 stars hidden throughout the over world – and within each level. Completing challenges would reward the player with a star – either by reading the endpoint of it or finishing a specific task. The actual over world itself would be locked behind different thresholds of stars; collecting enough stars in one area would allow the player to visit new levels. With each threshold came a special Bowser stage that required players to complete a level and defeat Bowser at the end.

The challenges themselves were unique to each stage for the most part. There were always two-star challenges per stage that were shared between them – collect 100 gold coins and collect the hidden seven red coins.

To officially beat the game, players just had to collect 70, while expert players could go for all 120 stars. An important reason for having a minimum number was that it allowed players of differing skill levels to at least see the ending of the game. In 2D design, you had to complete every level in the exact order to get to the end. With this design, if there were stages or challenges that you couldn't complete, you could still collect the required total elsewhere.

From a platforming standpoint, *Mario 64* would be the most evolved take in the series seen at the time. The game still had a control scheme centered around movement, jumping, and a general "action" command for Mario's controls, but the number of ways Mario could be manipulated were increased (which we covered in Section 6.4).

The variety of ways to move Mario around led to a phenomenon I've coined **subjective difficulty**, which we'll be discussing at length in the next chapter.

One of the more important aspects behind *Mario 64*'s evolution was a change in level design philosophy. In 2D games, levels were linear and required the player to perform exact jumps and motions to get through them the same way every time.

Given the wider space and number of ways to manipulate Mario, players were able to get through the levels with different techniques. This kind of design philosophy we're going to come back to in the next chapter, as it has become a staple of 3D platformer design. For lesser skilled players, if they were unable to perform a task, there was always something else they could do to keep moving forward in the game.

The number of power-ups was cut down to just three that were all based around wearing different hats – one gave Mario the power to fly, another turned him metallic, and the last one made him intangible and able to pass through certain walls. These power-ups were not designed around engaging with enemies compared to previous entries, but were about solving the various puzzles and challenges in the game.

Super Mario 64's design and impact are so great that we could dedicate an entire book just to it, but let's move on and talk about the rest of the industry.

11.4 The 3D Mascot Rush

Despite the Super Nintendo continuing to have games released, the mid-1990s began the transition into 3D for the console market.

As videogames became more cinematic, licensed games based on movies and TV would fall under the action umbrella, with games based on *Charlie's Angels, Hercules,* and many more.

For mascot-driven games, we saw both old and new mascots given the 3D platformer treatment. Older characters like Earthworm Jim, Sonic, Donkey Kong, and even Bubsy the cat were joined by newcomers like Spyro, Gex, and Banjo-Kazooie, to name just a few.

With rare exception, if there was a mascot platformer that came out during the 2D era that was relevant, a 3D sequel was going to be added to its franchise. With that said, we can talk briefly about some of the standout examples of 3D platformers.

Rare became known as one of the best developers working on 3D platformers outside of Nintendo. In 1998 they released *Banjo-Kazooie* which followed *Mario 64*'s formula, with the addition of having new abilities unlocked through play.

The Sega Dreamcast and Sonic the Hedgehog's first, but certainly not last, 3D entry was in 1999 with *Sonic Adventure. Sonic Adventure* mixed the traditional Sonic gameplay with exploration and puzzle solving. Playing as Sonic and other characters, each character had stages designed exclusively for them with unique gameplay mechanics.

Conker's Bad Fur Day released in 2001 also by Rare still stands as one of the few "Adult's Only" games to be released, and the only one in the 3D platformer genre. The game has achieved a cult status for its raunchy situations and gameplay variety.

In 2005, Traveler's Tales would begin their lucrative franchise of making Lego-themed licensed games with *Lego Star Wars*. Each game would be an action platformer based on a popular property aimed at children and family play. Since then, they have made games based on DC, Marvel, and many other properties.

Given the push to make 3D games, it was only a matter of time before developers would try 3D adventure platformers, and we did get to see some interesting entries.

11.5 Three D Adventure Platforming

The move to 3D gave a shot in the arm to adventure platformers. The greater focus on environmental design and exploration gave developers more room to come up with interesting and different challenges in the sub-genre.

The franchise that would become the standard for 3D adventure platformers was *Tomb Raider* released in 1996 by Core Design. In it, players controlled Lara Croft in a series of adventures. The objective was to guide Lara through different environments while avoiding traps and solving puzzles.

The bulk of the gameplay was built on puzzle platforming. Players had to figure out how to get Lara through or around obstacles using the environment around her. As we discussed in Chapter 9, the use of environmental puzzle solving would become a major part of 3D adventure platformers.

Unlike Mario and mascot-driven platformers, Lara's jumping was committed – jumping over large pits and climbing around structures to explore. There was combat that involved moving and jumping around while firing her weapons at enemies, most notably when she fought a T-Rex.

Instead of having progress tied to an open-world or collectible progression, *Tomb Raider* and other adventure platformers were designed with a linear structure – going from one level to the next. Players could find bonus treasures hidden in the levels, but they were not required to win.

The Tomb Raider franchise would have highs and lows until its reboot in 2013, and was turned into a third-person action-adventure game.

The Prince of Persia franchise had a lackluster first 3D entry with *Prince of Persia 3D*, but bounced back with *Prince of Persia: The Sands of Time in 2003*. Built on a combination of third-person combat and puzzle platforming, the series' original mechanic was the ability to rewind time.

As long as the player had enough of the game's resources available, they could rewind to avoid any damage or correct any jump. Following the game's fourth entry, the franchise has been retired since 2008.

Despite the evolution of adventure platforming in 3D space, much of the same problems that affected its viability in 2D were still around. You were still limited in terms of the variety of challenges, which is why combat was added in as a secondary mechanic. As we'll talk about in Chapter 13, this trend led to the AAA market moving away from platforming design.

Regardless of the genre, it's important to understand the differences that 3D brought to game design.

12

Three D Design

12.1 The "Depth" of 3D

Depth is the biggest difference between 2D and 3D gameplay. Players are no longer locked to one plane in terms of viewing the game space, and now have 360 degrees around them to explore.

Three D design is infinitely more complex than 2D. Not only do you need to design grander levels, but there is the increased work on art with designing 3D models. You cannot approach 3D game design the same way as in 2D. Earlier in the book we talked about the timelessness of 2D design and pixel graphics. The same can't be said about rough 3D titles that have not aged as well compared to 2D.

From an environmental standpoint, the environment needs to "make sense." Many 2D games feature level designs and architecture that, while they looked interesting, made no logical sense – stairways that lead nowhere, buildings that are maze-like, pits all over the place, and so on. This is often why designers will usually cite studying architecture for designing buildings that make sense.

Scale is another area that differentiates 2D and 3D design. A village doesn't have to be abstracted in a 3D space – you can literally build and model every structure, road, and piece of landscape. There is a lot more that goes into 3D design than we can fit into this section, and most of it is unrelated to jumping.

However, it's time to talk about the 3D camera, and why it has become a nightmare for many game developers to work with.

12.2 Three D Camera Design

As we touched briefly on in Chapter 10 concerning first-person cameras, the 3D camera is a separate entity when it comes to using it in a videogame. What that means is part of your UI must be set up to manipulate the camera at almost any time. Designers have standardized either the right analog stick or the mouse for controlling the camera with a gamepad or keyboard and mouse control scheme respectively.

In 3D design, there are several popular camera systems used in development; not all of them are suited for platforming.

The most popular style at the moment is the "behind the back" camera. Here, the camera is presented behind the character model and slightly above. This allows the player to keep the bulk of the character model at the bottom of the screen, only coming up to about the middle, while presenting the widest possible view in front of the character. The camera can usually be adjusted to show the character looking down and making it possible to gauge jumps.

The major disadvantage is that this camera tends to have trouble if a character is near a wall or too close to a larger enemy model, since it becomes difficult to see. The camera can get "stuck" in the model and prevent the player from seeing their character unless they move away from the offending object.

This is not the same as the "over the shoulder" camera system, which positions it so that the character is either on the left or right-hand side of the screen. This camera system is popular in horror and action games, and is oftentimes used for aiming and included in games with the behind the back style.

For platforming and combat that occurs 360 degrees around the character, an angled or isometric camera system is considered the best. This system allows the player to fully see their character model and their relation to the enemies and environment around them. The character model is kept positioned around the middle of the screen – allowing perfect vision of everything around them.

There are two disadvantages to this system. First, it is not good at showing the player what's in front of them or coming up. This can make it difficult if the player is moving too fast or trying to find something that is off camera. The other issue is that since the camera is completely separate from the character, it does require more work to get it positioned and adjusted properly.

Early 3D titles and those going for a cinematic touch would use fixed camera angles. Popularized by the *Resident Evil* franchise, the game could only be viewed by the angles chosen by the developer. Oftentimes this was used to hide key information to scare the player, and to cut down on the number of elements that needed to be rendered in the environment.

For platformers, when a section is especially tricky, developers will lock the camera to the best possible angle – allowing the player to only focus on the specific event. Otherwise, fixed camera angles are not popular in 3D platforming. If you put the wrong fixed angle in, it could make your game a lot harder – or even impossible – to play.

Many 3D action games tend to run into issues if they only present things at fixed camera angles, allowing the enemy to oftentimes attack the player off camera.

Due to the unique advantages and disadvantages of these systems, designers will often use several in a game to allow the player the best possible views of the gameplay. Many 3D platformers will allow the player to switch view styles: from isometric, to behind the back or first person, and allow further manipulation.

Because there are so many ways of adjusting the camera, many games will feature a "reset camera" command to bring the camera back to the viewpoint chosen by the game.

Game Design Deep Dive

One final detail is how moving a character in a 3D space works. Early 3D titles would make the direction pads or analog stick control the character in relation to their position. If you press "left" the character will start rotating left, and the only way to move them is by pressing "up." This is where the term "tank-like controls" came from and was a part of the survival horror genre.

For any kind of platforming, you want the control based on the camera's position, that is if you press "left" then the character will start moving to the left side of the screen. This is a more natural way of moving the character and is easier to process if the player has to perform multiple jumps while the camera is moving.

Another important feature is locking the character's movement independent of the camera until they change direction. In some 3D titles, if the camera changes while the player is moving, the character will change immediately based on the camera, often leading to the player moving in a way they didn't intend. By locking the character's direction, it makes it easier for the player to know where the character is going to be moving until they readjust things.

One of the major difficulties that happen in 3D platforming is being able to make proper jumps within a 3D space, and that takes us to a simple, but vital inclusion.

12.3 The Shadow Knows

The added plain and depth of field present in 3D creates a unique problem for 3D platformers. In a 2D space, the character's relation to where they are in the air and what's below them is easy to follow; the same can be said of first-person platforming. With 3D on the other hand, depending on the direction and angle of the camera, you cannot track where the character model is to the environment simply by the model itself.

Without having that reference, it becomes impossible to gauge any kind of jumping in a 3D space. The answer to this problem was simple: use a shadow to provide a frame of reference to the player.

Despite that simplicity, there are still several important factors to be aware of. The shadow must always be visible to the player when they are making any jumps. Some titles would have darker levels or special effects on screen that would hide the shadow.

If the player is making jumps from high up and there is no ground to cast a shadow, then the camera must be able to provide a viewpoint that can give them a frame of reference. The common solution was to position the camera behind the character's back, so that the player could see from the character's perspective where they were going. Another option is for the camera to look directly down onto the environment – or a top-down view. While it's not the most attractive way of showing off your game, it makes it very easy to gauge depth.

From our previous section we can see why having multiple camera systems is an important point in 3D platforming. Even with the behind the back camera, you still want to always show the shadow when possible to help the player.

One of the most frustrating platforming experiences I had in a 3D game was sadly *Epic Mickey 2*. This was due to the camera not showing a shadow, usually because the player was too high up, or not allowing the camera to go behind the back at specific points to provide proper reference for the player.

If you cannot provide any frame of reference in the 3D space for the player, then you will not have the capacity to design 3D platforming challenges.

Moving on, one advantage that 3D brought to game design was giving designers a chance at a new kind of difficulty curve.

12.4 Subjective Difficulty

The added depth that 3D brought to a title created a situation in which what I've coined subjective difficulty can occur. In a 2D title, the player is required to perform the same tasks and obstacles through a linear path. If a player cannot do the task required of them, then all progress would be halted.

In a 3D game, the open nature of the level design means that the same obstacles could be handled in different ways. Subjective difficulty is a case where the game's challenge is dependent on the player's skill level, and will rise or fall depending on how well the player has mastered the systems.

For the purpose of this book, we're only going to talk about how it relates to platforming, but another example would be learning the timing and mastering combat in the *Dark Souls* series.

Three D platforming is a great example of how subjective difficulty can be applied to games. With the 3D Mario titles, the games were designed to accommodate multiple skill levels, but at the same time, to help novice players improve.

There are two areas where subjective difficulty can be applied – via the level design and mastery of the game systems. The levels will have fixed goals or challenges to achieve, but the path through can differ based on how well the player is at controlling the character.

This is done by creating a game space that offers the opportunity to find shortcuts (either intentional or improvisational) through the obstacles. In *Super Mario Galaxy 2*, the first level was set up around basic platforming obstacles. As a new player you would perform regular jumps to get through the level, albeit on the slower side. Advanced players could make use of triple jumping and wall jumps to bypass entire challenges and get through it a lot faster.

Both strategies were perfectly valid, and you were free to progress at your own pace. As the game went on, the difficulty curve would increase in terms of the basic path through a stage. Later levels would "officially" introduce advanced jumps like the long jump, wall jump, and so on, even though those options could be used earlier in the game. At this point, a novice player would start to learn how to integrate those actions into their normal play.

By the end of the game, both the expert – and originally – novice players should have the same skills needed to finish the final sections. The beauty of this system was that the progression was still organic – the novices never felt like they were being rushed to learn the game, and the expert players would immediately be presented with challenges and situations suitable to their understanding.

A key element of subjective difficulty is how someone plays through the title will change as their understanding grows. In my previous book *20 Essential Games to Study*, I talked about how the puzzle game *Infinifactory* was designed to encourage players to return to previous puzzles with a new found understanding of how to play the game.

With the 3D Mario titles, once those novice players have gone through the game at the base level of understanding, they could repeat the game and play it entirely differently than their previous run.

While 3D platforming was growing, there is one alternative if you want platforming in your game, but not require technical skills.

12.5 Auto-Jumping

As we've discussed, jumping is one of the base mechanics of game design. Even if your game is not a platformer, the use of jumping to explore can still be a part of your title. For games that want to have that element, but not be about platforming, there is the system that we'll call "auto-jumping."

Typically in any platformer, the player must press a button to make the character jump, and if the player doesn't time it right, they will miss the jump. Auto-jumping removes the button press and makes the character automatically jump when they run off an edge of a platform.

The player only has a few ways of affecting the jump: determining the direction at the start of the jump, and sometimes having the option to abort it. One of the first examples of this system was in *The Legend of Zelda: The Ocarina of Time* and would be featured in all 3D Zelda games going forward.

The auto-jump is always set up to happen if the player is moving at a certain speed, usually if they are running. This is done to prevent the player from making the character jump when they don't need to.

While being easier to do than regular jumping, auto-jumping can have its own challenges. By removing the need to press a button, you can have multiple jumps occur in a rapid-fire motion – testing the player to direct the character in the right direction. Environmental puzzles can still be used with auto-jumping, and allow the player to focus on the puzzle or exploration as opposed to worrying about the platforming.

With that said, if your game is about testing the player's skills at platforming, then you don't want the game to take over and plot out jumps for them. This is why we don't see an auto-jumping option in 2D platformers.

Three D brought a lot of new elements to game design, but it wasn't long before the AAA industry began to move away from platformers.

13

The AAA Shift Away from Platformers

13.1 The Growth of the Game Industry

The platformer genre's popularity continued into the 2000s, but things began to slow down. Sega continued to try to make Sonic relevant with reboots of the design following the end of the Dreamcast, but none of them stuck. Each title following *Sonic Adventure 2* rebuilt Sonic's gameplay from the ground up with varying degrees of success and failure. Sony quietly moved away from having an official mascot and Naughty Dog stopped working on the Crash Bandicoot franchise.

With Microsoft's new system, the Xbox, the company did try early on to get a platformer mascot – with games like *Kameo* and *Voodoo Vince*, but the popularity of *Halo* became the new focus.

The only AAA studios still putting out pure platformers was Nintendo, and the 3D Mario titles continued to be some of the best 3D platforming around.

For the rest of the industry, times were changing. The mid-2000s was an important point when it came to the growth of the game industry. The increased power of the latest generation of consoles afforded developers the ability to create cinematic experiences. Hits like the *Final Fantasy* series, *Metal Gear Solid*, and *Uncharted* wowed gamers with polished gameplay and impressive graphics.

As we mentioned in relation to Halo, console gamers were now getting access to online multiplayers of their own; not a watered down version from the PC, but long-term supported multiplayers. The ability to play with your friends greatly extended the life of many titles, which was something platformers could not compete with.

Speaking of the PC, consoles were beginning to have the power to compete with the PC. Standardization began to happen with control schemes and UI design – making it easier to port games from the PC to console and vice versa. For a time, there were even talks about the PC industry dying and everyone just buying consoles.

At this point, I know some of you reading this are wondering when I'm going to mention the big game that came out during the 2000s. A lot of these changes and focus on mature storytelling could be dated to 2001 with Rockstar Games' *Grand Theft Auto 3* (or *GTA 3*). *GTA 3* was a watershed moment for the game industry.

There were mature games before this, but none like *GTA 3*. The game allowed players to fully explore a 3D city doing what they want, while following a brutal revenge story with professional actors voicing many of the characters. Despite the level of violence, profanity, and mature situations, the game showed developers and consumers alike that there was more that could be done with M-rated games.

One aspect that isn't talked about as much surrounding *GTA 3* was how it combined three different genres of gameplay – third-person shooting, driving, and third-person exploration – into one experience.

This would begin a trend of designers focusing on unified game experiences as opposed to being purely labeled by a single genre.

13.2 The Blending of Genres

A major shift in design philosophy occurred in the 2000s and into this decade. As game design evolved along with the technology to run it, designers began to combine elements of different genres together. Instead of a game just being a shooter, or a driving game, and so on, systems from other genres were introduced to provide more replayability or create a new experience.

Arguably the most popular (and profitable) was combining RPG progression and persistence in first-person shooting. The gameplay loop of powering up characters and unlocking new abilities over the course of playing was a cornerstone in the growth of the *Call of Duty* franchise, and soon became a core part of multiplayer shooters.

Platforming soon became a part of other designs, such as in the *Uncharted* and *Assassin's Creed* series. This is different from the era of adventure-based platforming where the platformer system was the core gameplay loop.

Jumping simply became a form of exploring the map instead of part of the challenge. You were jumping around to get to the next section where you would perform the main gameplay loop; usually combat or puzzle-solving. The mechanic of jumping was not a part of the challenge of the game. Many titles would introduce mechanics to even downplay the need of jumping – such as auto-jumping that we talked about in the last chapter. In this regard, we began to see the difference between a game that had jumping to it, and one that tested the player on jumping.

The obstacle and jump-based challenges we talked about in Chapter 7 were nowhere to be seen. AAA developers fully embraced 3D graphics and engines, and no one was making 2D platformers at that scale except for Nintendo and a handful of other studios. Three D design began to show the limitations of what you could do with platforming.

13.3 The Limits of 3D Platformer Design

In our previous chapter about designing a 3D camera, we spoke about the challenges that go into building an effective camera in a 3D space. It was a lot harder to create unique obstacles and platforming sections in 3D compared to 2D. With the additional cost in terms of time and money working in a 3D space, developers wanted to focus on what was popular, and the open world genre was the hot trend at the time.

Another roadblock developers were having with pure platformers was that they were hitting a wall in terms of how to create new takes on the genre. As we mentioned, *Mario 64* set the standard for 3D platforming, and it felt like everyone else was always chasing Nintendo.

Despite the freedom 3D brought in terms of environmental design, it proved to be harder to create technical challenges. The camera became a limiting factor, because if the camera couldn't keep up or show the right angle, then an obstacle could become unbeatable.

Despite the open nature of the game, platforming was reduced to linear sections

In our previous chapter about subjective difficulty, we noted how Nintendo was the only developer showcasing how to design platformers built around different skill sets, and it just kept them further in the lead compared to other developers. Platforming franchises like *Ratchet and Clank* and *Jak* would eventually downplay their platforming in favor of combat and exploration.

Nintendo's impact on platforming could arguably be another reason for the decline of the genre. While there were many 3D platformers, Nintendo continued to raise the bar in terms of design and gameplay, and no one wanted to compete against one of Nintendo's marquis franchises.

As the AAA industry embraced the "**games as a service**" model, platformers did not work with this model of continued development the same way that multiplayer titles did. A platformer is built purely on level design meant to be played solo. There was no way that a developer could keep creating content at that level and charge consumers for it.

When mobile gaming grew popular thanks to smartphones, we saw platforming come back, but in a simpler form.

13.4 Endless Runner Design

The idea behind an endless runner is that the character on screen is always moving forward (AKA running), and it's up to the player to steer them around, through, or above obstacles. The path the character is running on is procedurally built and designed to throw in harder obstacles and move faster the longer the character stays alive.

Despite that simple premise, there have been a variety of runners and runner-based titles released. One of the most famous examples didn't even involve running, but flying – *Flappy Bird*.

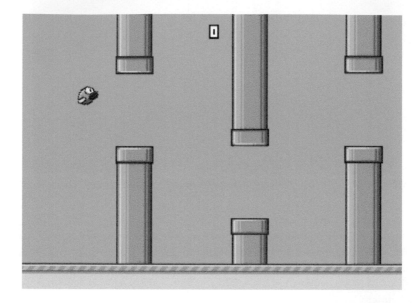

For this book, we're not going to spend a lot of time on runners due to the limited nature of the design. Since the character is always moving forward, it greatly limits the obstacle design and variety of gameplay. Obstacles usually only have one way to pass them, and messing up would send the player back to the beginning to try again. Some runners have persistence systems in the form of unlocking new content or costumes as they complete objectives or spend money.

Interestingly, Nintendo did try to create an elevated runner in the form of *Super Mario Run* in 2016. The game did not sell as well due to its high cost for mobile games and that it was still releasing 2D and 3D Mario games on their main platforms.

So far in this book we have discussed platforming and jumping from the AAA and AA market. However, some of the best and most advanced platformers released came from somewhere else.

14

The Indie Impact

14.1 The Indie Movement

The impact of **indie** development on the game industry could fill its own book at this point. For as long as there were major companies putting out games, there have always been smaller teams trying to create their own. Figuring out the exact date of when indie games appeared would be difficult due to the many games that were released outside of conventional methods. Early PC games such as the original *Ultima* were created entirely by game developer Richard Garriott.

From my own experience, I started to see indie games in the mid-1990s. Studios like Croteam, Introversion Software, Spiderweb Software, and more were creating titles their own way. Many early indie games were only available from the developer themselves, and this was a long time before there was any centralized source for buying digital games.

One of the most recognizable indie games to be released was also an action platformer with 2004's *Cave Story*. Developed solely by Daisuke Amaya, the game managed to deliver a great action/adventure tale without the need of a studio or team.

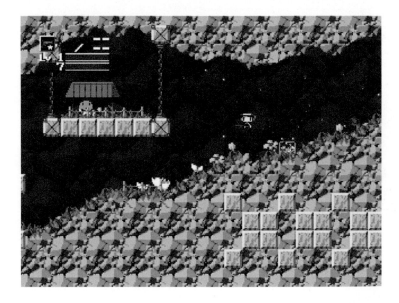

For the mainstream market, their first real exposure to indie development would happen with the Xbox summer of games event at the end of the 2000s. In order to market their digital store "Xbox Live Arcade," Microsoft promoted indie games from up and coming developers. The most notable at the time were *Braid*, *Super Meat Boy*, and *Fez*, each one a platformer with vastly different design. These three games and their developers were also featured in the documentary *Indie Game: The Movie*.

The popularity and widespread use of Steam provided a storefront for gamers to buy titles from developers all over the world, and led to the legitimizing of indie development and indie games. There is still so much we could discuss on the topic of indie development, but let's focus on their contributions to platforming.

14.2 Bringing 2D Back

In our previous chapter we talked about the move to 3D design shifting the focus among AAA studios. With developers focusing on big budget titles, this left a lot of room open for indie developers to work in 2D.

To say that indie developers picked up the 2D ball would be an understatement with hundreds of platforming-based titles released over the last decade. As we've mentioned, 2D is a lot easier to work in than 3D, and it became the perfect canvas for first-time designers and indie teams.

While there have been plenty of traditional 2D platformers, we have also seen developers trying to elevate the design in unique ways. Puzzle platformers like *The Swapper* challenged players to use clones to solve puzzles, while titles like *Thomas Was Alone* added storytelling beyond just jumping from point A to B.

We could spend a few thousand words detailing all the different mechanics and systems that indie developers have made use of over the last decade in 2D games. The important point was that the indie scene has kept 2D gameplay and design alive in a big way.

In other mediums, when a new standard is introduced (color TVs vs. black and white, DVD vs. VHS, etc.) the previous iteration is dropped in favor of

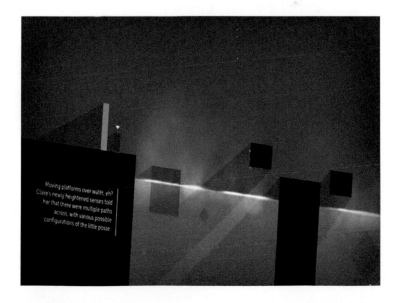

the new version. For a time, you could see the AAA industry trying to move away from 2D and phase it out for the larger studios.

However, the popularity of Nintendo's handheld line and the growing indie market proved that there were still heights to reach in 2D design. The limitations in terms of scope and technology that indies faced provided them with the perfect outlet for expanding 2D gameplay and storytelling.

In terms of aesthetics, there have been many indie developers who have pushed pixel graphics further than AAA developers did during the 1980s and 1990s.

One of the best examples of this indie expansion would be 2018's *Celeste*, which deserves to be talked about further.

14.3 Celebrating Celeste

Celeste is that rare platformer that blended storytelling, challenge, and accessibility all in one, which led to it winning numerous Game of the Year awards in 2018. From a platformer design standpoint, *Celeste*'s difficulty curve started out higher than other platformers, and only got harder from there.

The game wasn't physics-driven, but it did take into account the character's momentum that accompanied all jumps. The basic system relied on being able to jump, wall jump, and perform a dash in any direction. As we mentioned earlier in the book, when the player dashed, the momentum of the dash would affect the trajectory of any movement. Dashing before a jump would extend the length of the jump, as an example.

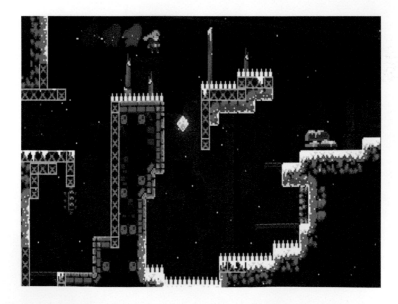

Knowing when to dash and how it would affect your momentum became crucial as the game went on. Each stage featured unique environmental obstacles and challenges to get through. The environmental obstacles were used to create unique sections within each stage that were one-offs for that stage. Beating the game at the basic difficulty would be a challenge for any gamer, but there was more to it.

Featuring two additional difficulties of levels, the game demanded a lot out of a player if they wanted to do everything. Harder stages would require the player to learn new ways of combining the dash and jump. Instead of *Celeste* only being known in hardcore circles, the game was celebrated for being open to everyone.

The reason for this was down to how the developers handled accessibility by allowing the player to adjust the difficulty outside of the game design. At any time, the player could turn on a number of options that would radically reduce the difficulty of the game. These included infinite dashing, increased jumping, and invincibility.

The player was never pressured or rewarded around their use of these systems. If someone wanted to beat *Celeste* without them, they would find one of the hardest commercially released platformers in 2018. On the other hand, the game could be the absolute easiest for people who just wanted the story.

The story was tied into the plot and accessibility about providing a game that anyone could enjoy without feeling like they're playing it wrong. The heroine suffered from depression and anxiety attacks, and the plot was about her overcoming those feelings and learning to be a better person because of it.

The important element of *Celeste* in terms of difficulty balance was that the accessibility options were not factored into the design of the stages. *Celeste* was

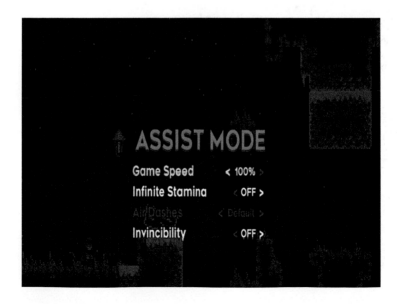

balanced around expert players, but became open for anyone to enjoy. The accessibility options were akin to a wrapper outside of the gameplay – and mattered as much or as little as the player wanted.

Celeste, and many other indie platformers, helped to foster this idea of a "modern retro" market.

14.4 The Modern Retro Market

"Modern retro" is a term that has gone to define titles that are made today, but have the look and feel of older games. Some designers take this literally and try to create some of the hardest titles. Other designers use the old school aesthetic and design as a jumping off point to try and create original games that exceed the games that they copied.

While these games may look like a NES or SNES title, they often feature enhanced graphics, different gameplay modes, and more. One of the best examples of this would be the hit *Shovel Knight* developed by Yacht Club Games.

The title has the look and feel of a long lost NES game, but the developers put their own spin on the design. The game featured original levels and mechanics that paid a little homage to the classics. At the same time, the game was modern in terms of its accessibility – offering frequent checkpoints and providing players with bonus challenges and rewards.

At the time of writing, the game has had two successful expansions adding in new characters that had completely different mechanics, and a third one along the way.

Another favorite is the developer Locomalito who has put out original titles inspired by retro games. One of his most famous was *Cursed Castilla* that was a homage to *Ghosts N' Goblins*, but was built from the ground up as an original title.

As with Yacht Club Games, there have been developers who did unique mechanics within the retro environment. *Odallus the Dark Call* by Joymasher is the only 2D game to my knowledge that used a double vertical UI instead of a horizontal.

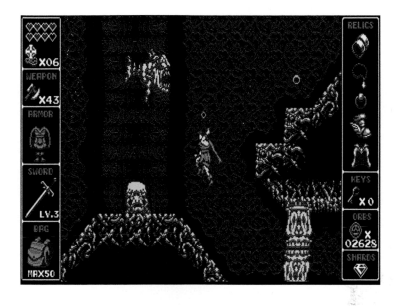

There are countless more examples of indie developers who have used retro design in this fashion. In earlier chapters we talked about why 2D design is not going away, and the modern retro market is proof of it. For the truly dedicated, there are after-market companies that put out their own versions of classic hardware, complete with cartridges you can buy and use in retro consoles.

As with all genres, there is a wide margin between successful modern retro games. If you don't understand why retro games worked and only focus on the difficulty, you're not going to have a successful game. A lot goes into successful retro design – not just with platformers – that would be too far off topic to get into here. In Chapter 17, we'll talk more about difficulty design which hits many areas of game design.

The indie market pushed platforming design in ways that the AAA developers never did, and created a more complicated form of platformer.

15

Physics-Driven Platformer Design

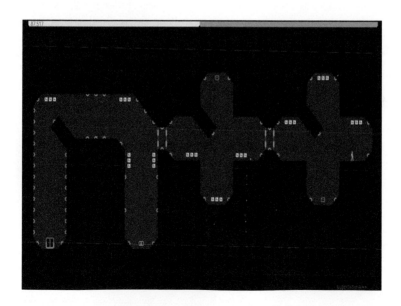

15.1 Incalculable Jumping

In our previous chapters discussing 2D design, we talked about how early games would feature preset jumps based on the variables discussed in

Chapter 6. For basic platformers, the levels and obstacles were designed and balanced around only a small number of jumps the player could perform. This also had the side effect of keeping things simple in terms of level and obstacle design.

In order to create higher skill challenges and design, indie developers began to use what we'll call "physics-driven platforming" to greatly expand what a player could do. When we use the term "physics" in this way, it's kind of a misnomer. Every action-based title ever made has its own internal physics regarding how characters behave. All the factors we talked about in Chapter 6 were always different in every game.

With physics-driven platforming, a character still has a minimum and maximum jump distance, but the jumps in-between are not locked. When we say that the jumps are "locked," we're referencing the developer hardcoding any and all possible jumps within the game. In a physics-driven platformer, every minute movement the character makes will change the trajectory of their jump. The game is constantly monitoring the character's velocity and momentum and using that to create jumps. Not only that, but if the character is being pushed or gaining extra velocity in some way, they can gain additional height when it gets applied to the jump. In this way, it is almost impossible to calculate the number of jumps a character can make in a single game.

Sonic the Hedgehog was the first time a AAA developer made use of physics-driven platforming, but my first exposure to it on the indie side was the N series by Metanet Software. Now up to its third iteration, *N* looks simple from the outside – your mission is to reach the exit in each stage while collecting gold.

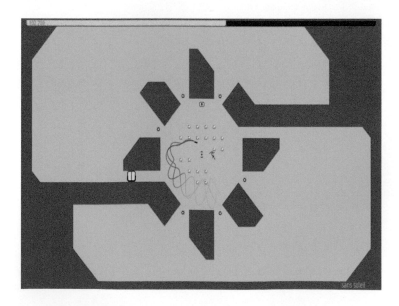

Where the difficulty comes in is guiding your character (a ninja) through the stage with your momentum constantly being factored into jumping, running, and most importantly dodging. Many stages featured jumps or sections where you only had one chance to do it right, because you would not be able to regain the velocity to make a second attempt.

Earlier we touched on *Super Meat Boy* during the Microsoft promotional campaign. *Super Meat Boy* also featured physics-driven platforming, but was more focused on obstacle design. Every stage had elements that the player had to avoid, or would impact the momentum of the titular Meat Boy.

Even though physics-driven platforming allows for the same obstacle and enemy designs as traditional platformers, they do require a different focus on level design to make them work.

15.2 Technical Level Design

Physics-driven platforming is about presenting a highly technical challenge to the player. Due to the freedom the player has in controlling their character, basic pits and traps will not be enough to present a challenge.

The focus instead becomes about presenting an obstacle that requires the player to perform a specific set of actions to get around it. Earlier in the book we talked about the term micro-adjustments to describe the player constantly altering the character's trajectory while in the air.

Physics-driven platforming will often challenge the player to steer and readjust their character multiple times per second to pass an obstacle. Due to the increased focus and challenge, the pacing of levels will be different compared to traditional platformers.

Levels as a whole will be shorter to run through (once the player knows how to get through it), and there are far more checkpoints. With the game *Celeste*, every room was its own unique challenge that tested the player in different ways. It would be unfair to the player to require them to memorize multiple solutions at the same time and punish them to repeat content if they failed. Going back to the *N* series, every stage was only one screen long and designed around a single core obstacle.

Fighting enemies or solving puzzles are not usually seen in these kinds of platformers, as the focus is put on the technicality of movement. If there are enemies in the game, they will either have to be avoided, or used in service of the platforming. In the title *Dustforce*, players would attack enemies to carry their momentum across gaps.

The amount of focus and skill required to play physics-driven platformers or just technically focused ones makes them popular for speedrunners to show off. At that level of play, finding the best way through a stage is akin to racers trying to find the perfect line through a course.

Physics-driven platforming has evolved the design of jumping, but it's not without some considerations to keep track of.

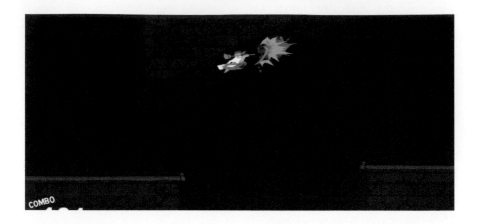

15.3 Physics Problems

While there have been many platformers released in the indie space, physics-driven platformers only make up a small subsection of that. With the focus being entirely on the platforming, it does limit the design and audience.

People who play physics-driven platformers want a challenge and aren't interested in a story for the most part. Due to the higher skill level involved, these platformers can be rough for new players. The technical skill required to play them can cause players to hit a wall that they may not be able to get past. In the last chapter we talked about how *Celeste* used accessibility options to mitigate the challenge in it, but most physics-driven platformers focus on just the hardcore experience.

In terms of camera placement and tracking, you need to make sure that the camera can move fast enough to track the player's position at all times. In the game *Dustforce*, there were several sections where the player, having their velocity increased, would move so fast that the camera could not keep up in time. This led to sections where you had to react faster than the camera in order to make it through safely.

Ultimately, the issue that hurts the long-term play of physics-driven platformers is that they are very hard to design new and interesting challenges around. The high skill level required to play them from the start quickly assimilates players with the kind of obstacle and environmental design the game will use.

Unlike titles that introduce new mechanics or systems, these kinds of platformers are limited due to the degree to which the player has control over their character. There are only so many ways that you can make a jump over a pit interesting. Once you master the rules and advanced maneuvers required, the designer can't create anything new to challenge the player without adding in brand new elements or gameplay.

And if the player can't figure out the maneuver needed, then they would become stuck at the game. Going back to *Dustforce* for a minute, the entire game's progress was about mastering the stages in order to unlock harder stages. If the player can't get the best ratings on the levels, they would not be able to make any more progress at the game.

In this way, physics-driven platformers tend to be on the short side once the player knows what he or she is doing. Even if the game comes with a level editor or continued support, without new elements or obstacle design, an expert player will not be fazed.

This is why we have seen developers focus on a limited number of ways of manipulating the character, and then coming up with creative options to test the player's mastery of the character. For that, we turn to the rise of player-created levels and the Kaizo sub-genre.

16

Super Mario Maker and Kaizo Culture

16.1 Making Mario

One of the most surprising games released on the Nintendo Wii U was *Super Mario Maker*: a game aimed primarily at giving players the ability to create levels in the styles of *Super Mario Brothers 1, 3, World*, and *New Super Mario Brothers*. Despite the industry's growth over now 30+ years, there have been very few games released with a focus on letting players design levels without needing a programming background. The previous example would be the hit series *Little Big Planet*, and if we wanted to go further back, there was *Klik and Play* in 1994.

Super Mario Maker was, and still is, a big deal among game design. The entire program works without letting the player look at – or create – computer code. Instead, Nintendo used the iconography of the Mario franchises as shorthand for explaining what everything does.

If you've played any of the Mario games in *Super Mario Maker*, then you knew the logic behind every object you can put in your level.

Nintendo expanded their functionality by allowing the player to combine and alter items and characters in ways that were never in the original game. This also meant creating new forms of obstacle design and challenge; all tied to the Mario formula.

Following the game's release, Nintendo released several content patches meant to add in new obstacles and allow designers to create challenges never seen in a traditional Mario game. Some examples would be the use of

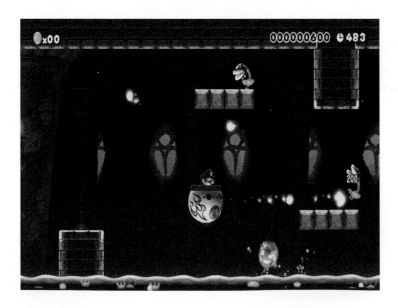

checkpoints in older Mario games, red coin challenges (collecting red coins to unlock a door), and as we're about to discuss, some of the most fiendish levels ever created.

Before and just after the game's release, the general thought was that creators would simply create traditional levels built on Mario's formula over the years. Nintendo invited many high profile game designers to create their own interpretation on a Mario level. However, they quickly transformed *Super Mario Maker* into something that no one was expecting.

The *Super Mario Maker* UI gave players an unprecedented amount of detail when it came to Mario's jumping and momentum. You could see the pixel-perfect velocity behind every jump, test every section, and create levels as big or as small as you could dream.

With that newfound freedom, creators soon turned things up to 11 ... or maybe 200, in terms of difficulty. At this point, trying to examine all the levels designed in *Super Mario Maker* would be impossible. The game has a feature where you can send people your levels based on a code, or follow people so as to always view their stages.

This has opened the door up for another form of content when streaming videogames on YouTube or Twitch. Well known creators have streams of them designing levels or playing the hardest levels out there.

When I say the word "hardest," that is not hyperbole. There are levels that are made up of nothing but pixel perfect jumps, speed runs where you only have 30 seconds to clear a stage, puzzle stages that can take hours to clear, and many more.

For casual fans, they would see this in the "100 Mario challenge" mode. In this mode, the game pulls a random assortment of levels based on their overall clear percentage. At the highest difficulty known as "super expert," the levels that can show up could have clear rates less than 1 percent. You only have 100 lives to clear all the stages, and it's very easy to go through them.

Levels that simply focus on design fundamentals or emulating the same things seen in the original games aren't as popular these days. *Super Mario Maker 2* was released in the summer of 2019, and it didn't take long for creators to push the difficulty and designs using the updated editor.

The extreme levels of difficulty have created polarizing opinions when it comes to quality. Many of the hardest levels designed have no rhyme or reason to them, or any considerations towards platforming philosophy. In our next chapter, we're going to talk about that line between challenge and frustrating gameplay.

As we said at the start, there have been previous attempts at introducing non-programmers to level design, and even an unofficial *Mega Man Maker* available, but Mario continues to be the go-to for creating levels, and that bears further investigation.

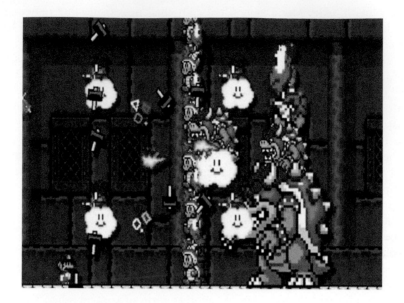

16.2 The Legacy of Mario

Super Mario Maker continues to highlight Mario's longevity when it comes to platforming design and why it's considered to be the popular template for Kaizo levels. From a historical standpoint, *Super Mario Brothers 1, 3,* and *World* are some of the most recognizable platformers ever made.

In turn, it reduces the learning curve needed to understand what's going on. Part of the reason for *Mario Maker*'s popularity was the fact that someone didn't need to know programming in order to start building levels. It doesn't take long for someone to understand what a goomba does or what the fireflower power-up does.

The popularity of these titles also meant that there were plenty of copies available for people to examine, which we'll be coming back to in the next section.

From a design point of view, all three games aren't that hard to play, but they do have a wide range of elements that can be tweaked. By using obstacles or items in unique ways, they open up the door for creating unique levels and situations that Nintendo never put into a Mario game.

One of the first such examples of this was an early *Mario Maker* level that tasked players to actively avoid super mushrooms in order to complete it. Designers were not adding in new elements to *Mario*'s design, but simply using what's there in a different way.

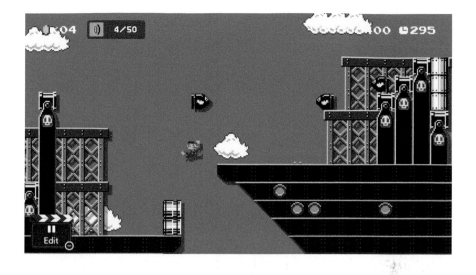

Even though *Super Mario Maker* would become known for overly difficult levels, designers were simply copying a style that has existed underground on the internet.

16.3 What Is Kaizo?

Since the 2000s, there has been a style of platformer design that has existed away from mainstream consumers. Kaizo is a Japanese term that has become adopted by the community and has been translated as "reorganize" and other synonyms. The general concept of a Kaizo game is focusing on extremely challenging levels and situations that you would never see from a mainstream game. The **skill ceiling** for a Kaizo game easily puts other titles to shame.

The first known example of this kind of game being recognized was the title *Kaizo Mario World* in 2007 after footage of it was posted on YouTube. Kaizo games are considered "hacks" of the respective game they're based on. In the last section I mentioned how widely available the original *Mario* games were in terms of physical copies.

Many early modders would take the files off the cartridge for distributing – or pirating – the game to the PC. A discussion over piracy is a serious part of the game industry, but far too big a topic to discuss here.

Nevertheless, taking and modifying these files has allowed modders the ability to create patches that can be applied to the game and make it run the specific Kaizo hack. There is now an unofficial software specifically designed to edit and create *Super Mario World* hacks that has streamlined the process.

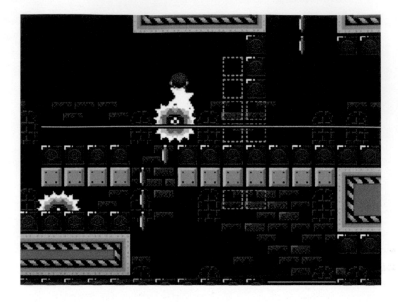

Regardless of the hack and modder, as we already mentioned, Kaizo games are all built on a similar concept of difficulty. The level designs in a Kaizo game are always on the expert side. Back in Chapter 7 when we described the different kinds of jumps, Kaizo games always combine jump types into very challenging sections.

A level in a Kaizo game is typically split into two difficult sections, both making use of different obstacles to challenge the player. There is no break between obstacles, as the player must perform each section in its entirety on a single run or be sent back to the start or checkpoint.

An infamous element of Kaizo games is the concept of a "kaizo trap." A kaizo trap is an obstacle that will kill the player if it gets triggered, but there is no way of knowing where a trap is unless it gets sprung. A basic example of this is an invisible block set up along the easiest jumping trajectory to clear a platforming obstacle. To avoid it, the player must purposely jump at a different angle while still clearing the obstacle.

Despite the difficulty, it hasn't stopped players and modders alike from embracing these Kaizo games. Some of the most popular Kaizo hacks have original **assets** made exclusively for them. With that said, due to the fact that these titles are run on modified game files, they will never be made available for commercial sales on any storefront. Likewise, I legally cannot mention any places here as to where to find them.

While Kaizo hacks have become associated with *Mario*, there is another series I want to briefly touch on.

16.4 I Wanna Be a Platformer

Another Kaizo game that debuted back in 2007 was *I Wanna Be the Guy* (or IWBTG). While *Kaizo Mario World* was a hack for the game, IWBTG was original in terms of structure and gameplay. The game did make use of assets taken from other games, and was more than happy to mix up elements at any time.

Each screen was loaded with traps of both the regular and Kaizo variety to kill players. Their only means of preserving their state was with checkpoints put in-between sections. The player's only mechanics was jumping and a shot for attacking enemies and bosses. Unlike *Kaizo Mario World*, IWBTG did feature originally designed boss fights that were homages to classic games and characters.

This is another game that became an underground hit as word spread about it. There were a few direct sequels made by the original creator, but it has since become its own subgenre with fans making their own takes on the IWBTG formula. Some takes focused more on fighting bosses, others emphasize the platforming; and there are many other examples. At this point, there

are too many of them out there for us to break down in this book, which could easily fill another Game Design Deep Dive.

Despite these games never being sold or featured on major stores, their popularity and notoriety has increased this decade.

16.5 Bringing Kaizo to the Masses

The popularity of Kaizo games and levels in the mainstream market has grown with the continuing awareness of **speed running**. A biannual event known as Awesome Games Done Quick, or AGDQ, has done a lot to show off speed running culture while donating to charity.

At each event, speed runners show off ways of beating the games in the fastest ways possible. Sometimes this is through only skill, other times they will use glitches and exploits to utterly crush a game. At some point, someone needs to write a book chronicling the rise of speed running culture if there already isn't one out by the time this book is published.

As AGDQ grew in popularity, it soon began to be picked up by major sites and mainstream audiences. At each event, there is usually a block of time dedicated to Kaizo games due to the amount of technical skill required to play

This is from my (brief) world-record speed run of *Cuphead* after the game's release

them. While it may take hours to master, or even just beat a Kaizo game, experts can play them in far less time.

Given the popularity of Kaizo now, some may think that there is a market to develop a commercial Kaizo game. However, the design has some important considerations we need to be aware of.

16.6 The Limited Appeal of Kaizo

Kaizo-based gameplay has such a high degree of technical skill required to get through it that it greatly limits the audience. Many Kaizo games will eschew modern game design and structure in favor of the high difficulty.

The **progression curve** in a Kaizo game is different from traditional games and represents a specialized form of gameplay.

For lack of a better term, we're going to classify this as **mechanical gameplay** and define games that are built on a singular way to get through them. This kind of design was popular with early console games and attributed to the higher difficulty back then.

Classic titles would make use of fixed trigger events and scripting when it came to enemy AI and obstacle design. Instead of you fighting an enemy or boss that would be directly reacting to your actions, you would fight something with a **fixed pattern**. Expert players would learn how to exploit these patterns to essentially make enemies and bosses do what they want.

In terms of design, this meant that obstacles would behave on a fixed timer in terms of where elements would be on screen or within the level itself.

Given the fixed nature of mechanical gameplay, it becomes possible to program an AI to go through a title in the most optimal way possible. This is where the concept of a "tool assisted speed run" or TAS come from. The AI is capable of performing actions faster than any human could input them, and often leads to crazy runs being done.

The problem with mechanical gameplay and by extension Kaizo design is that there is no room for anything but the perfect play. You're not reacting to the game, but performing a precise set of actions again and again until you get it right.

This is why even the best Kaizo players out there will still have hundreds of deaths when they're playing a new game for the first time. An interesting element of mechanical gameplay is that these games don't have a progression curve. While the skill ceiling is obviously higher, you're not playing a Kaizo game in the same way as other titles.

In a traditional videogame, the progression through a title will introduce new elements to challenge the player and make them become better at it. Each new level will build upon the previous to keep presenting new things and test the player's knowledge.

If someone finishes *Super Mario Odyssey*, they will be a far better platformer player at the end than they were at the beginning, because the game continues to test their abilities. Such a player could go back and play through the game again – or go for the post-game content, and find that they're playing it at a higher level of skill.

In a Kaizo game, while each level has the same platforming foundation, they feature sections and obstacles unique to the individual level.

Learning the best way through one stage means nothing when you are playing a different stage. It's all about execution and memorization, which aren't transferable elements. Going from one stage to the next is like starting back at zero in terms of figuring out what to do. What's worse is when a level makes use of a technique or mechanic that you're not good at. It is very likely that the majority of people who pick up a Kaizo game will hit a wall when the game asks them to perform something they can't do.

The closest a commercially released game got to being a Kaizo title that I'm aware of would be the indie game *1001 Spikes*. Each stage required the player to memorize the patterns of obstacles and perform a perfect run to get through it.

Earlier in the book we talked about subjective difficulty and how it allows different skill levels of players to progress through a game. Mechanical gameplay is the complete opposite of it, as there is no room for anything but the one way to beat the stage. We could also point to games that feature randomized or procedurally generated content and situations as another counter-example to mechanical gameplay.

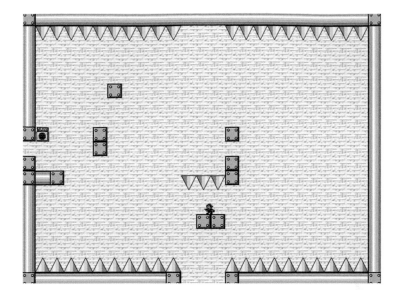

Modern games tend to make use of more randomly generated or less scripted content. This is why it would be a lot harder, or even impossible, to set up a TAS for modern games when there are less opportunities for a set pattern.

17

Expert 2D Design

17.1 Level Philosophy

Level design is a multi-faceted topic when it comes to game development – every genre has its own rules, examples of good and bad designs, and more.

To keep things focused, we are only going to be focusing on platforming design. One area that we will not be talking about is building a Kaizo game, as we already discussed how it is a sub-genre of platforming and not one aimed at commercial markets.

When it comes to building a platformer, there are three key areas in my opinion that should be considered.

What's the Theme?

Every level in a platformer needs a theme or mission statement. Do you want to make a level based on bouncy jumps? Do you want an underwater level? How about one long set of Kaizo traps? Having a theme is an important point about platformer design, as it's very easy to go overboard. It's better to have one focused theme in your level than just putting down every idea that you have at once.

Many *Super Mario Maker* levels that are criticized will try to just overwhelm the player with all manner of objects, sounds, and effects going off. By adhering to a theme, you are focusing your thoughts on making one level the best it can be, as opposed to going all over the place.

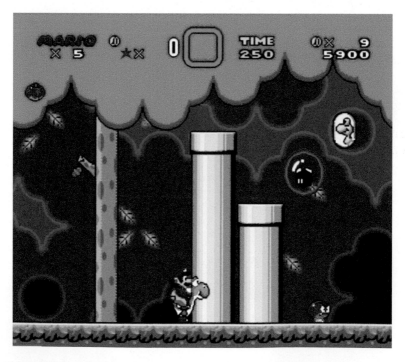

Each area in *Super Mario World* affected the level designs, obstacles, and more

Even Kaizo games, despite their high difficulty, will stick to a similar concept with their level designs. Oftentimes, a Kaizo level is two distinct sections tied by a theme or obstacle.

Another advantage is that if you start coming up with ideas that don't fit within the current theme you can use them for another level.

Progressing

Great level (and by extension game) design will always have a sense of progression to it. The challenges in the level should grow harder the further the player goes. This should always culminate with a final challenge – a boss fight or the hardest section.

The ideal difficulty curve of a game is that each stage grows progressively more challenging to go through, but you shouldn't always keep escalating the challenge. For example: if stage 3 has a difficulty rating of 3 out of 10, stage 4 shouldn't immediately start at 4 out of 10, and so on.

The problem is obvious: you are going to run out of ways of making the game harder without providing a balanced challenge. Instead, try to introduce new elements, or reintroduce older elements in a new way.

Despite the number of levels in *Super Mario Brothers 3*, the game only has a few levels that would be considered hard to play. Instead, what the developers did was use the theme of each world as a starting point and experiment with different level designs. It didn't take long for the player to understand all the mechanics of platforming, and could instead focus on each level's unique elements.

Another major point about progression and difficulty is that you also have to take into account the player's understanding of the game. The further someone gets in a title, the harder it will be to keep providing challenges due to their growing skill level. At some point, one of two things will happen: the player will become so good at the game that nothing in it will challenge them, or they cannot improve anymore and hit a wall that will force them to stop playing.

The former is something that you cannot stop, and the latter leaves a bad impression for your game. We'll be talking more about having challenging levels in the next section, and difficulty balance is a topic that goes beyond just platformers, and will show up in later books in the series.

As you start building your levels, you should have an understanding of the skill level of the player you are aiming for. A game that is aimed at expert players from the get-go would start with harder levels that would be a challenge for them. If you want to appeal to a greater audience, then you want to design your levels to ease players into the gameplay.

One other aspect of progression is allowing the player to maintain their progress through a level. In most platformers, the more checkpoints you have

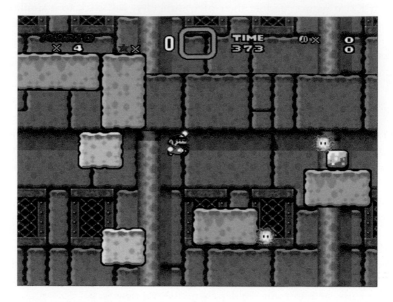

The *Mario* games tend to throw in more elements at once to test the player near the end of the game

in a stage, the easier it is to go through. Longer stages should have at least one checkpoint to save the player's progress.

If during **playtesting** you find players are getting stuck at a particular section, place a checkpoint before and after it. You don't want someone to keep repeating content they've already finished to get back to where they're struggling, and the checkpoint is a reward to let them know that they've gotten past it.

Knowing When to End

The final point is one that has frustrated many designers – understanding when to end a level. Good level design is built on a "quality over quantity" philosophy. Going back to the first point about themes, your level should make use of everything that you wanted out of the theme you've chosen. The more ways that you can test the player on a specific theme, the more you can add to the level. There is one important rule you must follow: you should never repeat the same exact challenges in a single level. This is viewed as "padding" your game out and is frowned upon by gamers.

Lesser platformers will repeat the same obstacles multiple times in a row or throughout a level in an attempt to increase the size of a level. A level should only be as long as the number of *unique* ways that you can challenge the player. You can repeat obstacle design at a higher level further in – making a kind of "final test" for the player. As long as the situation is not exactly the same, you're good.

The *Mario* games have all been great examples of this, and have only gotten better with later iterations. Every stage has something new added to make it stand out from everything else. The levels are only as long as they are to make use of the new element in different ways, and then it's over.

On the other hand, the game *Voodoo Vince* frequently repeated sections and challenges to pad out the experience. The simplicity of the mechanics meant that the player reached mastery early on, but must still repeat the same elements: sometimes in the same level.

Speaking of elements, we need to talk about what it means to create the ways the player will interact in the game.

17.2 Creating Mechanics

Creating mechanics in a platformer falls into two groups: how the player interacts with the character and how the character interacts with the environment.

Starting with the first group, as we mentioned, the main form of interaction in a platformer is obviously jumping. We've already spoken about how to design jumps back in Chapter 6, but I want to focus at least briefly on what it means to create and decide on what mechanics you want in your game.

With platformers built on jumping as the core gameplay loop, you need to make sure that the act of jumping feels right in the player's hands. What we

A good mechanic or element is one that can be used in a variety of situations and challenges

haven't discussed in this book is having additional mechanics like attacking, wall jumping, and more.

Even though the act of jumping is going to be your main system, you must still make sure that any other mechanics can be used comfortably with it. From a UI standpoint, it's important to understand the difference between a primary action and a secondary one.

Primary actions are mechanics that the player is going to be using constantly – jumping and running for platformers. Secondary actions are mechanics that are conditional to specific events – wall jumping, throwing an item, picking something up, and so on.

Primary actions should always be assigned to separate buttons on a gamepad or keys on a keyboard, to reduce the chance of hitting the wrong action. You need to be careful with how your UI is laid out to make sure that the player can comfortably use all the mechanics in your game.

The player should not have to shift their hands around to reliably play your title. If the player must make use of two or more actions at the same time, make sure that it is easy for the player to do so. One option is to set actions that are meant to be used in unison so that both hands must be used. This way, the player can better associate an action to one of their hands, and not have to worry about the same hand hitting multiple buttons at once.

For secondary actions, you can make them **context sensitive** so that they are only triggered when the game calls for them.

Given the skill intensive nature of platformers, you want to do your best to limit the number of buttons the player needs to use in a game. Many platformers

have tied secondary commands to button combinations: in *Castlevania*, the player will use their sub-weapon by pressing "up" and "B" at the same time.

To make it easier for the player to remember these commands, try and associate them with similar actions in your game. The *Castlevania* example works because the player already knows that B is used for attacking, and then it's just one additional button press.

The other side of the equation is mechanics that are explicitly tied to the environment. This can be anything from hitting switches to controlling vehicles and more. The *Super Mario* series still remains one of the best examples of creating a variety of mechanics through environmental design.

Controlling Mario doesn't change, but by adding new hazards, items, and situations, they continue to keep the game interesting from start to finish. The more mechanics in your title means that you have a greater pool of elements to draw from when designing new levels or sections.

There are two points to keep in mind whenever you add in a new mechanic to your platformer. The first goes back to our previous section and concerns making sure not to pad your game out. The best additional mechanics in a game add depth to the design and can be used in a variety of situations – such as wall jumping.

If you come up with something that would take a lot of additional time and work to add, but it only makes sense for a few minutes of gameplay, then it may be better to focus on mechanics that you can get more mileage out of.

The other point is that the more additional mechanics you add to your platformer, the more you "dilute" your core gameplay loop. Always keep an eye on whether or not a mechanic can be tied back to your platforming. Many platformers do feature **mini-games** or sections that don't involve jumping to break up the gameplay. If those sections are required to progress, they can sometimes be viewed as taking away from the rest of your game if they come up too often.

What's worse is if the new mechanic was not integrated well into the gameplay – such as having an impromptu stealth section in an action game. If someone buys your game for its platforming, they may not want to spend an hour driving around on a map.

No matter what you add to your game, everything will factor into the difficulty of your title, and that takes us to one of the hardest topics to discuss.

17.3 Challenging vs. Frustrating

Difficulty in a platformer, as with most action-based titles, is ultimately based on the player themselves. When you're designing your title, keep in mind that you will have players of all skill levels looking at your game: from people who have never touched the genre, to masters who have beaten the hardest games.

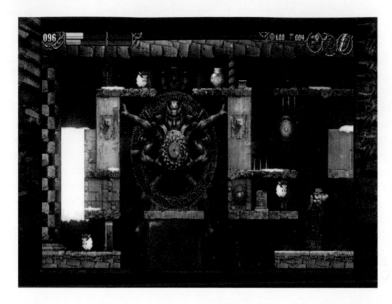

The *La-Mulana* franchise is known for its brutal difficulty as part of its appeal to fans

There is a greater discussion to be had about difficulty than we could fit in this book. Many expert players feel that difficulty is equal to quality in all walks of game design. The infamous phrase "git gud" has been tossed around whenever discussions regarding challenging games happen.

There is a fine line between a game that is challenging to play and one that is considered "cheap." In this instance, "cheap" refers to games that are designed intentionally to frustrate the player through its design or UI.

Another aspect is if the difficulty is there just to frustrate people instead of providing a unique challenge. Going back to *Super Mario Maker*, you could design a five-minute-long level of nothing but pixel perfect jumps where any mistake requires the player to restart the whole thing.

Getting through it would be difficult, but would the player actually grow or improve their skills or knowledge by playing it? Another debated case would be the use of Kaizo traps and what they represent.

A Kaizo trap is something that no one can truly prepare for, as there is no on-screen indication when there is a trap, and no amount of skill will allow someone to avoid a trap. A common theme of frustrating games is when the player loses and it's not their fault. Sometimes it's because the game was purposely set up to introduce a high **difficulty spike** out of nowhere. Other times the game trains the player to do X, and then without warning punishes them for doing so.

Ultimately, it should always be the player that's the reason why they succeeded or failed at any challenge in your game. With that said, getting the player to the point of understanding that is difficult no matter what the genre is.

It takes a lot of skill as a designer to balance difficulty in your game. It's very easy to create levels on either extreme, either for novices or expert players, as it's all a matter of tweaking the variables.

If you want to make a jump very hard, turn it into a pixel precise one; if you want to make it easy, reduce the distance to the point that any jump would clear it. A great designer can make a level that provides new and expert players with something unique for them to try.

One of Nintendo's skills as a game company has been creating titles that fit for a wide audience of skill levels. Every *Mario* game has a difficulty curve to it, but Nintendo knows that they have expert players wanting more. As far back as *Super Mario World*, there have always been bonus stages designed at the absolute hardest the team could devise. These levels may unlock something extra for winning, but they are never required to see the end of the game.

That last point is important, as you want to be mindful of a player hitting "the wall" – or when a player cannot move forward due to a lack of personal

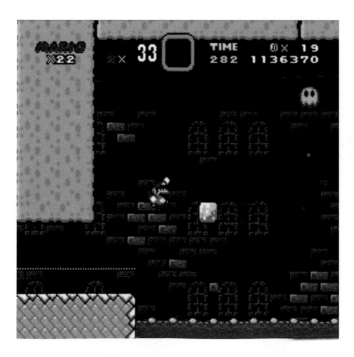

In this scene, a player would have to make this tough jump, or have a far easier time if they found the respective "switch palace"

skill. For platformers, because of how player skill is factored into the design, you cannot just take a section and easily create different versions of it based on difficulty. For titles where they expect the player to grow over the course of playing, if someone cannot figure out an earlier section, skipping them ahead would simply get them stuck at the next one.

An area that Kaizo games – and titles that only cater to hardcore players tend to fail at – is providing a learning curve for players. Back in Chapter 7, we talked about how it's important to teach the player new rules and mechanics.

If you're going to feature original obstacle design in your game, then you must try to teach the player about it before hitting them with hard examples. This is where organic level design shines in cutting down on the difficulty of a game. Just by playing through the stages from beginning to end, a player will learn the mechanics and obstacle design of your title.

You cannot assume that your player base knows obstacles and techniques from other games. Some of the hardest Kaizo titles will use glitches and techniques that have been discovered over the years and many of them will not reference what they are or how they work. While Kaizo is again an extreme example, any techniques or maneuvers that are required to beat the game should be formally explained by the design.

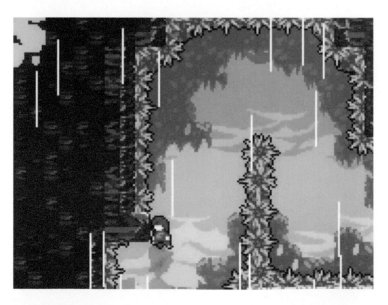

The "wall dash jump" maneuver can be done at any time in *Celeste*, but the game waited to formally introduce it

Going back to *Celeste*, there were advanced maneuvers that players could have used from the very first level that the game didn't reference. The reason was that the levels were designed around not having to make use of them, similarly to the subjective difficulty discussion we had earlier with *Super Mario Galaxy*. The game waited until the additional difficulty levels arose, when those maneuvers then needed to be introduced to the player.

If you want to guarantee that people will be able to finish your game, you can look at accessibility options like the ones we mentioned in *Celeste* back in Chapter 14. Starting with *Super Mario Galaxy 2*, Nintendo has been adding in assist modes in their main franchises. A second player can provide backup to someone who is struggling – usually a parent helping a child out. For their platformers, if someone fails at a section too many times, they can turn on a special assist item that removes any penalty of failure until the end of the level.

Our final point for this section is the importance of playtesting. If you're trying to aim your title – no matter the genre – at a specific audience, then you need to get feedback from them. Skill-focused titles like platformers in particular need to be carefully balanced. Testers will be able to comb over every inch of a game in ways that the designer would never have the time to do.

Understanding how to conduct proper playtests is beyond the scope of this book, but you want to pay attention to any "pain points" in your levels. A pain point for our purpose is a section that players get stuck at for a long time, or just end up quitting your game at.

As already mentioned, there are many ways to make something easier or harder; even the addition or removal of one platform can completely change a section. The only way you'll be able to figure these things out is to have people examine your level design.

Moving on, another element of design that any good designer needs to comprehend is how collision detection works.

17.4 Collision Detection

The use of hitboxes are vital in any game that makes use of **collision detection**, and the implementation and design of hitboxes are too many for this book to cover. To make sure everyone is on the right page, a hitbox is an invisible box defined by the designer around the character model.

The hitbox is the game engine's way of knowing when objects collide with each other. Enemies and enemy attacks will typically have a hurtbox, which is simply a hitbox that determines if something has been hit and should report damage. When it comes to platforming, we're focusing on the size and shape of the hitbox and how it affects jumping, avoiding hazards, maneuvers in the air, and landing.

In most of the early 2D titles, the character's hitbox was not designed perfectly around the character model, or in other words a 1:1 mesh – this was

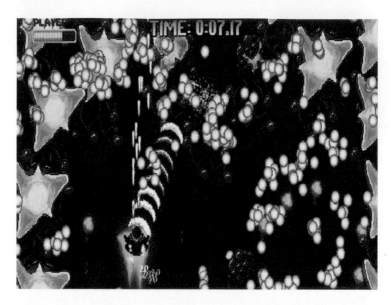

Many "shmups" are designed around pixel-precise movement and hitbox understanding

most likely due to technical constraints. Instead, developers would place the hitbox to cover what players would consider to be hitting the character. Given the improvements in game engines and technologies, many modern titles do have hitboxes shaped to a character's body.

This is often why obstacles or attacks that just barely touch a character's model may not register as a hit, because the two hitboxes did not come into contact. As a quick aside, understanding hitbox positioning became a vital element of the shoot-em-up or "shmup" genre. For people who speed run videogames, understanding the hitboxes on a character model can lead to discovering specific bugs or glitches they can exploit while running a game. Some famous examples would be from *Super Mario 64*, and allowing Mario to go through specific walls, break event triggers, and much more.

Depending on the action at hand, the hitbox's size and shape may change. For platformers where characters can jump on enemies, a hitbox around the feet will detect if the character lands on an enemy's hitbox and defeat them.

A basic form of collision detection is how the game engine will always be checking for whether the character's hitbox is colliding with any surface that is considered "ground." This is how the game checks for whether the character is either in the ground or in an aerial state, which we examined in Chapter 6. For 3D titles that have "invisible walls" to prevent the character from leaving the game space, the game uses the character hitbox to detect and stop the character.

Game Design Deep Dive

For platformers that made use of grabbing ledges or interaction points, the character's hitbox would have to connect with the part of the object in order for the character to interact. Grabbing interaction points should never be hard or frustrating. A lot of the difficulty comes down to how the character jumps.

If there are only a few ways of jumping in your title, make sure that the interaction points can be easily accessed. Earlier in the book we talked about committed jumping and how hard it was sometimes to hit floating items or power-ups due to the fixed angles.

When it comes to jumping, we've talked about how the game should be constantly checking for whether the player is touching the ground or in the air. If the game's engine isn't checking fast enough, you can run into situations where the character can jump despite not touching the ledge. The reason is that the game hasn't done the check yet, and still thinks the character is on the ground.

With that said, we have seen platformers in the past leave this element in as a hidden trick, but you don't want to base obstacle design on it. The reason is that it's not something that would be made apparent by simply playing your title, and players may not know that it even exists.

An important function of hitboxes is when it comes to avoiding obstacles and hazards. You must always be aware of the safe way through the obstacles in your game. Ultimately the hitbox will determine whether or not the player has made it through unscathed. You want to avoid solutions that require the player paying more attention to the hitbox than the character model.

The character's hitbox is the sole judge when it comes to avoiding obstacles and dealing damage. Any changes to the size or shape of the hitbox must be reviewed carefully with the rest of your design.

A major case of how a hitbox can impact everything came with the *Crash Bandicoot N Sane Trilogy* released in 2018. The *N Sane Trilogy* was an attempt by studio Vicarious Visions to remake the original three titles by Naughty Dog for the modern era. This included redesigning the entire game around a new 3D engine and building new assets to accommodate everything.

With the *N-Sane Trilogy*, Vicarious Visions used a "pill-shaped" hitbox for collision detection, for which I'm assuming the original used more of a square shape. Because of the rounded edges of the hitbox, it made it easier to slide off edges if the character barely makes it on. Fans found that this also led to increasing the jump distance if you performed Crash's slide and jumped at the right moment.

However, I ran into a separate issue that occurred near the end of the game. During one of the game's final sections (which you can see in the screenshot), the player needs to perform a jump over an environmental hazard while a laser beam is fired from above.

By increasing the size of Crash's model and changing the hitbox, this simple maneuver became a lot harder to perform. Crash is so big now that a regular jump will have him hit by the laser. Jumping too low would cause Crash to touch the hazard and die that way. In performing this section about 30 times, only once was I able to jump high enough to clear the obstacle while avoiding the laser and not taking damage.

Crash Bandicoot features a mechanic where if the player dies enough times at a single section, the game will provide them with an "Aku-Aku mask" that grants one free hit of damage. For anyone who reaches this section in the *N-Sane* remake, I can only assume they got through it using the mechanic or already having a mask from earlier.

Returning to 2D design, it's often considered frustrating design to create sections that rely on hitbox manipulation. What that means is intentionally designing a section that requires more attention to the character's hitbox than their model. For platformers, this could be requiring the character model to stand in a hazard to make a jump, but technically be fine because the hitbox did not connect.

No matter what kind of platformer you are designing, you must also be mindful of collision detection. Any changes to the size or shape of character or environmental models must have their hitboxes adjusted to accommodate.

17.5 Tracking Timers

For our last topic, I want to briefly discuss the concept of timers and how they relate to level design. A unique element of level design when it comes to platforming is the fact that you have multiple obstacles moving around at the same time. In order to keep everything synchronized, developers will make use of timers to keep track of where elements are.

A section will be designed around a repeated loop of time; usually a few seconds at most. Within that loop, platforms or elements that the player will come in contact with will be repeating the same **cycle** of actions.

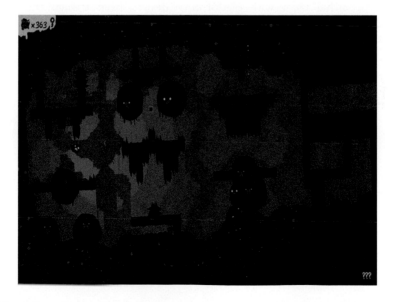

In this section, the moving platforms have had their movement synchronized

When the timer is up, that simply means that the elements would have returned to their original position to restart the cycle again. Without player interference, the cycles and their elements will keep repeating.

If you don't think about timers, you can run into situations where sections are out of alignment and it will be impossible to predict at the time if the section can actually be completed. Another problem is if the design didn't properly test the loop of time – what ends up happening is that the correct path may only show up one time out of ten cycles of loops. Not only does this slow down the game, but will lead to wasted time if the player must repeat the section.

There are two kinds of timers used: global and local. A local timer means the cycle will not start until the player and the camera reaches that section. A global timer is when all the cycles that will take place in a level are running regardless of the player's position.

Local timers are easier to manipulate on a case by case basis, which means that it is possible to find the perfect path through a level, knowing where everything is at one time. From a design point of view, you need to be careful about a local timer becoming misaligned if the player only triggers part of the cycle when they reach a section. Having only one part of the section activate will completely mess with the timing until the player reaches another section.

Global timers once set up will allow your level to run like clockwork. For 3D titles where the level design is not locked to the camera, global timers are standard.

Depending on the secondary systems in your game, there is a lot more that goes into pairing them with platforming design. Even though there's too much to talk about with this point, don't be afraid to combine elements, as you never know what combination could spark a brand new gameplay loop.

18

Conclusion

Whenever I think about game design as a field of study, it reminds me of something a developer I interviewed said: "Game design is the combination of entertainment and programming." You need to understand both in order to create a videogame.

This is why I wanted to write this book and why platforming was a no-brainer as our first topic. No one has had a discussion about the act of making a character jump off the ground at this level of detail. As long as people are designing videogames, there will always be another platformer ready to make you jump and dodge your way through levels.

With just this genre alone, I don't think I've ever written this much on a single topic at once before writing a book, and that's for good reason. Many people view platformers as just being simple, and yet it's one of the easiest genres to mess up at the design level. I hope that you all took away the complexities and intricacies and have a new respect towards game design.

Thank you so much for reading this book and I hope that this is the start of many more Game Design Deep Dives to come.

Glossary

2.5D: A kind of style where the game will be designed around moving in 2D, but features a 3D character and environment.

Assets: A blanket term to describe any aesthetical elements in a game.

Camera: How the player views what's going on in the game. There are multiple variations based on 2D and 3D design, and depending on the respective genre.

Character: Who the player is controlling in a videogame.

Checkpoint: An in-game save point placed by the developer to preserve the player's progress.

Collision detection: How a game engine decides any character's relation to everything else in the videogame.

Committed jumping: A form of jumping design where the character can only jump at fixed velocities with no further input from the player.

Context sensitive: An action the player can do that will only trigger when it is applicable to the gameplay.

Core gameplay loop: The primary mechanic and/or system that a videogame is about.

Cycle: Describes a loop of actions that are repeated by the elements in a level, which are then set to a timer to repeat.

Difficulty curve: A term to describe the rate of the game growing harder over the course of play.

Difficulty spike: A term used to describe when a game becomes a lot harder and at a faster rate compared to what went before it.

Environmental puzzle: A form of puzzle design where the puzzle itself is about moving through the environment of a game instead of relying on items or puzzle-solving to get through.

Fall damage: A mechanic where the character will take damage or die if they fall from a predetermined height.

First person: A form of gameplay typically used in shooters where the camera represents the character's vision and the player is looking through their eyes.

Fixed pattern: Also known as a set pattern, when an enemy or boss in a game is designed to repeat the same attacks and motions regardless of the player's actions.

Games as a service: A term that describes videogames that are meant to be sustained after release via continued development and in-game purchases.

Gamespace: Another way to describe the environment around the character.

Hitbox: An invisible box or wireframe around a character model that is used to determine collision detection in a game.

Hub: A non-linear area that connects to all the levels in a videogame.

Indie: Shorthand for "indie developer." A person or team making games without a major studio or budget behind them.

Isometric: A viewpoint in videogames where the camera is looking down and at an angle at the game space, giving a 3/4 perspective. Can also be used to create a faux 3D look.

Kaizo: Can mean "rebuilt" and other synonyms in Japanese, but has been adopted to stand for brutally difficult games; usually those based on hacked or modded titles.

Mcguffin: A colloquial term to describe an object that is the focus of a story.

Mechanic: A term used to define actions or verbs that the player can make use of in a videogame.

Mechanical gameplay: A way of describing a game that is designed around having a set experience and a limited number of options that will beat it.

Metroidvania: A genre where the character gains new abilities over the course of playing that change how they respond or behave.

Micro-adjustments: A term to describe making minute changes to a character while they're in the air to either avoid hazards or safely land.

Mini-game: A section in a title that features a completely different gameplay loop for a short experience. Typically used as a change of pace or as a reward.

NPC: Stands for "non-playable character" and describes any character in a videogame not controlled by a player.

Organic tutorial: A way of designing a tutorial that teaches the player without stopping the flow of gameplay by using the level design itself.

Platformer: A genre of videogames that typically focuses on jumping as the core gameplay loop.

Player: The person who is playing the videogame.

Playtesting: Having people outside of the game's development team to examine a title and weigh in on what they think about it.

Power-ups: An item that can either appear randomly or is directly placed by the designer to provide some kind of benefit to the player.

Progression curve: A way to describe how someone grows over the course of playing a title, either by becoming better at the game or having their character grow stronger.

RPG: Stands for "role playing game" and describes a title where characters become stronger via abstracted systems.

Section: A collection of obstacles the player must clear before reaching safety. Can be one screen or multiple screens of obstacles.

Skill ceiling: Used to define the maximum skill level someone has when it comes to playing a title. If the game's difficulty is higher than the player's skill, then they will not be able to beat the game without assistance.

Speed running: The act of playing a game in the fastest way possible. Can be done via exploiting in-game bugs and glitches, master level play, or a combination.

Subjective difficulty: A term to define titles where the difficulty is dependent more on the player's understanding of the design instead of just by the level and obstacle design.

System: In this situation, the term is used to define a collection of mechanics that all operate together. For example, all the different kinds of jumps in a platformer would fall under the jumping system.

UI: Stands for "user interface" and represents anything the player uses or needs to experience a title. This includes on-screen elements to the control interface.

Variable jumping: A jumping system that allows for multiple kinds of jumping based on specific variables.

Index

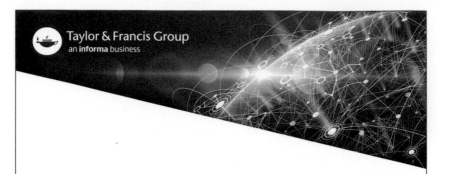